# 'DON'T JUST STAND THERE. DO SOMETHING!'

— Dick Dastardly

Published by The Do Book Company 2023
Works in Progress Publishing Ltd
**thedobook.co**

Foreword and editorial selection
© Miranda West 2023
Text © individual authors
Images © individual photographers
and artists, see credits p287
Cover artwork © James Victore 2023

A CIP catalogue record for this book is
available from the British Library

ISBN 978-1-914168-15-4

The authors featured in this book are
donating the 10% royalty to charities
supporting literacy and environmental
causes. More details on our website.
A further 5% is given to The DO Lectures
to help it achieve its aim of making positive
change: thedolectures.com

To find out more about our company, books
and authors, please visit **thedobook.co**
or follow us **@dobookco**

Cover designed by Tom Etherington
Book designed and typeset by Ratiotype

Printed and bound by OZGraf Print on
amber graphic, an FSC® certified paper

10 9 8 7 6 5 4 3 2 1

# The Book of Do
## A manual for living

DO
Book Co

**Each of us is given the same number of hours every day, but some people make more things happen in the same time. Why is that?**

Well, they have learned an important, and yet mostly untaught, life skill. They have learned how to go from 'talk' to 'action'.

They have discovered the secret of 'Doing'.

# Foreword

Ideas can be powerful. Our book company was one such idea. After watching a DO Lecture online back in 2011, I sent an email to the founders asking if they had considered publishing books by their speakers. A response came back and, a year or so later, a new independent publishing house came into being.

Our intention was to publish 'books that inspire action'. Concise guides that focused on the 'doing', not the background theory. To encourage us to reach our potential, to improve our lives and the world around us. Over the last ten years I hope that, in some small way, our books have achieved this.

*The Book of Do* brings together excerpts and images from across the collection of nearly 40 books (and counting!) to create a 'manual for living' that provides wisdom and advice on how to live a fuller and more sustainable life, work smarter, or even take a different path. The themed sections include Change, Ideas, Work, Team, Creativity, Sustainability and, of course, You.

This book celebrates a body of work from a host of talented and pioneering Doers. It features words from those who have 'been there, done that' — who we now have the privilege of calling our authors, even friends — and images from some of the most thoughtful and creative people out there, including our long-standing cover artist, James Victore.

It's funny, magical even, how an inanimate object like a book has the power to change lives. To make us get up and move, start something, have new ideas, change direction.

We hope something exciting lies in store for you.

Keep reading and doing.

**Miranda West**
Founder & Publisher
The Do Book Co.
London, 2023

# Introduction

Is your seat comfortable? Good. Do you have
a refreshing beverage to hand? Smashing.
Then shall we begin our journey? Fantastic.

This book that you're holding in your hands will be your all-in-one
guide, ticket and passport to your new destination. Where exactly
are we going? Well, I'm not sure, that's for you to decide...

We can arouse your curiosity to discover a new hobby or set
you on a path to a brand-new career. Maybe this is your first time
flying solo and the choice of places to visit or paths to follow is
overwhelming — fear not, I'm here to help guide you.

What I'm getting at in this ridiculously metaphor-laden
introduction is about you, the lovely reader, going on a 'journey'
(sorry for the *X-Factor* lingo), finding what you love and making
that your focus. Your ultimate goal is to blend what you enjoy doing
and what you get paid to do, so they're one and the same.

Madness, right?! Work is 'work' and the fun stuff comes once
you've left for the day. Nope, it doesn't have to be that way. It's totally
possible to find or create a job you love that encapsulates all your
passions and interests. It's also totally possible to find a new vocation,
do a total 180-degree turn and start afresh. We all deserve the
chance to discover and fight to do the things that make us happy.

Words from *Do Fly* by Gavin Strange

Have you noticed that you have more ideas
when you are not thinking about the thing you
should be thinking about? Umm.

# THE CREATOR'S CODE

1    **Find your love.**
2    **Spend your life at it.**
3    **Trust your instincts.**
4    **Ignore doubters.**
5    **Chase the work, not the money.**
     **(The money will come.)**
6    **Use your ideas to push this world forward.**
7    **Don't let your ideas down: Execute well.**
8    **Work with great people.**
     **They are not always the easiest.**
9    **There are no shortcuts. Do the hours.**
10   **Great coffee helps.**

# THIS BOOK IS ABOUT DISRUPTION

It's about doing things differently.
About having ideas that will change the world.
That will at least change your world.
It's also about delivering those ideas.

Having ideas is easy. The difficulty is making them work.
The block can be confidence, befuddlement, inertia, money,
knowing where to start.

It's easy to say but you just need to start.

This book will help you create ideas and it will help you
do things differently. Hopefully it will make you happy.

# PREPARE

# Getting fit for your purpose(s)

Part of being agile is the ability to bounce back when events knock you for six. In sport, in work, in society, in relationships — you name it, life has setbacks, usually just when you don't want them. To quote Claudius in *Hamlet*, 'When sorrows come, they come not single spies, but in battalions.' We need strong defences to cope, and move on. And mental resilience is one defence we all need.

The American Psychological Association (APA) defines mental resilience as the process of adapting well in the face of adversity, trauma, tragedy, threats and sources of stress. Simply said, it is about having the mental strength to deal with pressures and challenges.

Psychologists are in agreement that to build mental strength you need to focus on an individual's ability to build a sense of control of their own emotions — and have confidence in that control. This, they say, is rooted in people being comfortable in their own skin and, crucially, in having a life purpose. Having a life purpose means they are sure of who they are and have a strong moral code that gives them a clear perspective on events unfolding around them. They can be confident their response will be aligned with this code and take strength from the knowledge they are doing the right thing. Self-respect then follows.

The basic building blocks of good health — exercise, diet and sleep — are also vital in building mental resilience. Meditation can also be helpful. These all help build stamina (both physical and mental) and the balance of mind that aids perspective. Gratitude, too, can be an important element in resilience. Being grateful for the good things you have going for you is a strong antidote to losing your peace of mind.

Also high on the APA list is fostering a positive mental attitude. It's worth noting that when you take up a positive attitude, its opposite doesn't automatically dissipate. It still takes effort to avoid strength-sapping and debilitating pessimism. Pessimism leads to learned helplessness. The reverse of resilience.

Despite having to sell my company, Cobra Sports, for £1, I had been confident in my purpose. That purpose had been to build a chain of sports-shoe shops that achieved two aims. The first was our broader company aim: to get more people participating in and enjoying sport by providing highly informed and trustworthy advice to customers on the right shoe for their needs (gait, pronation, and level of seriousness). Although it's hard to believe now, there were no shops that did this, and certainly none on the high street. The second aim was more personal: to have highly trained and articulate staff to provide that trustworthy advice. A team that could be proud of their expertise and the help they were giving.

Twenty years after Cobra Sports folded, my daughter was wearing an old sweatshirt with our logo splashed across the front. The security guard at the shopping centre she was headed for stopped her as she approached. She was slightly worried, but he soon reassured her, explaining that he'd worked for us. He said it was the happiest and most motivating job he'd ever had. I like to believe this was because we had a purpose — one shared by the whole team of 200 employees.

# Adapting purposes

It had been a worthwhile purpose, and it had worked.

But it was no longer relevant to me, as the business was gone. It taught me that life events mean adapting one's purpose and refocusing in response to those events.

If you have already known your purpose from a very young age, and it's one that will stay the course, you can treat this chapter as revision. If not, you are far from alone. Indeed, most people find that over a lifetime their purpose adapts to the values that are relevant to them at the time, usually in response to life events. Having a purpose that adapts and alters is not unusual and can be a more attainable prospect than finding 'one true calling' and sticking with it.

It is the reason for the plural 'purpose(s)' in the chapter heading. Far too much emphasis is placed on finding your one true purpose and it's incredibly unhelpful. It puts too much pressure on finding that one glistening gem and hinders you from seeing the multiple ways you could feel fulfilled over the course of a lifetime.

The crucial thing is to make sure any adaptations are made within the overall framework of your long-term moral principles and (as we shall see, within that) the values most relevant — and motivating — to you.

The focus of my subsequent purpose evolved slowly. But over time, I have refined it to: 'helping people get insight into their situation so they can be more effective and fulfil more of their potential'. All the activities I now pursue — and have done for over two decades — are underpinned by this purpose. Whether it's writing books, speaking at conferences, running CEO think tanks, or being actively involved in charities, they are all aligned with my purpose. It's not tidy and precise, but it's accurate and true. Above all, it motivates me to keep on working well beyond conventional retirement age.

# A strong moral code

**There comes a time when one must take a position that is neither safe, nor politic, nor popular, but we must take it because conscience tells us it is right.**

— Martin Luther King

What has helped me significantly through the vicissitudes of being self-employed, with no monthly salary cheque and other challenges along the way, has been the key element — confirmed by the studies into mental resilience — of possessing a strong moral code.

My moral code is based on honesty, compassion, fairness and kindness. They may sound like good, wholesome values, found in any mushy fairytale, but they can be very hard to live up to at times. Let's look at why I try to live by them.

## Honesty

Being honest with yourself is just as important as being honest with other people. This is especially true with work. I well remember working with a company who hired an alarmingly ruthless chief executive, who subsequently spent time in prison. I had to deal with someone working for him who had accepted his code of morality. He tried to convince himself that living by one set of values at work, and another set in his private life, was OK. It's not OK, and never will be. Eventually the double standards destroy the integrity of the individual. Conscience monitors honesty, and ensures honesty is something you feel in your belly as much as understand up in your head. It is central to being agile — without it you are in danger of being nimble, but having no solid basis to move from, or to. And without solid and sustainable foundations, you won't feel grounded. Most importantly, it is vital to futureproofing — a dishonest construct for a future is one likely to implode through lack of substance.

## Compassion

Compassion means not only being sympathetic to suffering, but having a desire to alleviate it. This is especially relevant to one of the major trends of the last decade, namely a growing tendency to see the less fortunate members of society as scroungers, whose misfortunes are self-inflicted, rather than the result of poor housing, lack of education and poverty. This is partly driven by self-interest and selfishness — an unwillingness to share resources — and partly by ignorance — a lack of understanding and empathy for those suffering deprivation and the reduction of the little support they had.

Conscience again comes into play. We feel as well as know that action is required to be more compassionate, whenever we get the opportunity.

## Fairness

Life is not fair, but that doesn't mean we have licence to behave unfairly. Fairness again has its roots in conscience. We feel, as well as know, that if fairness underpins our actions they will be just, and we will be able to act without guilt. It should govern all behaviour, because unfairness is not only unjust, it ultimately destabilises society, so we all lose.

## Kindness

Whereas compassion is about being empathetic to human suffering, kindness is the generous response to human beings around you. It is often insightful — foreseeing someone's discomfort before it happens. It is about being proactive in a good-natured, benign and affectionate way. Not to put too fine a point on it, it is about love.

Kindness is hardwired into our evolution as a species. As a result, kindness produces dopamine and oxytocin in our bodies — the so-called happy chemicals. Each act of kindness can also boost the immune system, increasing resistance and reducing anxiety.

Not all human beings are endowed with sufficient milk of it, making its scarcity of great importance.

Things don't always go right, particularly when you're responding to change at speed. I find being grounded in these four principles gives me resilience, and having a purpose to guide me provides a more enhanced mental fitness to cope. Challenges and setbacks can be easier to deal with if they are seen in the wider perspective of the worthwhile journey you are committed to.

So there is a lot to be said for identifying an inner excitement and commitment that will drive efforts to deliver over the long haul. Which poses the question: where will I find that meaning? A purpose that will be the source of my enthusiasm? Something that will make things happen, day in and day out?

## Finding your purpose is not a race

There are many issues involved in defining a purpose. One is our natural mindset. Do we have a proactive or a reactive mindset? Do we respond to events, or do we pioneer new solutions to problems before others even perceive them? Is our locus of control internal, or do events control us?

The truth, I suspect, is messier than psychologists would have us believe. And the important thing is not to worry if you find you have no overwhelmingly meaningful point of focus for your emotional and intellectual engagement. There is no hurry to be first past the finishing line in finding a purpose. Indeed, as we saw above, some elements of the finishing line may morph over time.

For those — like me — who are slow to alight on a focused passion, it may take not only time but many versions, diversions and a few cul-de-sacs to find it. This is normal, and should not cause concern. The important thing is to learn from the journey towards — and through the manifestations of — purpose. And not to be dispirited by the dead ends you may encounter along the way.

In simple terms, finding a purpose means finding something you enjoy. Not just doing pleasant things with pleasant people (though that can help), but trying things you feel instinctively will give you a buzz when you do them. And something that is satisfying. Satisfaction of this kind is more important than short-term happiness, which comes and goes and doesn't tend to be long-lasting. Satisfaction and fulfilment, on the other hand, tend to be more substantial. You can have setbacks, bad days or even weeks, but if you find what you are doing fulfilling, it's somehow OK, and you press ahead.

In terms of the work you do, it should — if at all possible — be aligned with your purpose. We spend so many of our waking hours working that it makes sense for work to be the start point for the journey. That's true whether you are looking for a career readjustment or replacement, or just a sizeable side income.

There are many worthwhile issues and challenges to address. Finding the one most relevant to you at this point in your life is where to focus most energy. And a sensible starting point to help work out what that might be is to look at your values.

## Values

To clarify, values are different from morals and principles. The latter are unchanging. My core principles of honesty, fairness, compassion and kindness don't change with circumstances. They are not relative to the situation I find myself in.

But values, by necessity, adjust to your life events.

Tidiness, for example, may be something you value, but once you have young children it may have to take a back seat for a time. Being financially well off may be important at one time in your life, but adopting the mindset of Living on Less may see financial reward dropping way down your list of the key values to focus your life around.

Which is why agility is so important. As what you value adapts, you may need to spring nimbly to your new cause or be accepting of a new reality — while not taking leave of your core principles.

# Start mapping

Understanding your values and embracing their flexibility will give you real insights into who you are at this point, who you aspire to be, and where you might look to find more meaning in your life. It is a mystery that is never quite solved, and that is part of what makes life so interesting. Just as you will change over time as life events add to the richness of your character, so too will your values change.

In order to highlight and, importantly, to prioritise your values, the first step I suggest is to create a values map. This can take time, and considerable thinking about. Don't rush it. Here is a list of values to start with. There are likely to be values that are important to you, but are not included in the list — if so, add them.

Accountability
Ambition
Behaving morally
Being competitive
Being creative
Being liked
Belonging
Broad vision
Care for the environment
Caution
Compassion
Control
Co-operation
Courage
Creating value
Dialogue
Domain balance
   (physical, emotional,
   mental, spiritual)

Efficiency
Empathy
Enthusiasm
Fairness
Family
Flexibility
Focus
Forgiveness
Friends
Future generations
Gentleness
Harmony
Helping others
Honesty
Humour / fun
Image (how others see you)
Independence
Insight / understanding
Integrity

| | |
|---|---|
| Interdependence | Responsibility |
| Kindness | Reward |
| Knowledge | Security |
| Learning | Self-discipline |
| Love | Self-improvement |
| Meaning | Serving the community |
| Nutrition | Social responsibility |
| Openness | Status |
| Perseverance | Tradition |
| Personal development | Trust |
| Physical exercise | Wealth |
| Pride | Wisdom |
| Productivity | Work / life balance |
| Respect | |

Having selected your list of values that are most relevant to you, now take time to rank them. You are aiming to get to your top ten values in order of significance that you already do, or intend to, live by. All the values on the list may seem worthwhile, but their importance, deep down, to you is what you are looking for.

The list intentionally includes my four principles of honesty, fairness, compassion and kindness. This recognises that the categories of what constitutes a value and what constitutes a principle are not rigid. Importantly, it gives you a fix on where they are now in your values hierarchy.

When you have refined your personal list to identify your top ten, you will probably find one or two of the values near the top of the list that are not getting a fair share of your focus and energy at the moment. They are important to you, and you haven't been paying enough attention to them. This will give you insight into how your life may need to change to accommodate this.

Over time, I suggest you make two lists. The first, and most important, is the list of your own values. And the other is the list of the values of your current workplace, if you have one. If there is a considerable difference between the two, which is possible, this in itself will be enlightening. It may indicate you need to relocate to a workplace more in tune with the values you want to live by.

My list of values has changed as life events have had their impact over the years. During the early years of the sports-shoe business, my top five values were:

— **Integrity**
— **Enthusiasm**
— **Creating value**
— **Humour / fun**
— **Physical exercise**

Having lost the business, got married and then had two young children, they changed to:

— **Family**
— **Integrity**
— **Helping others**
— **Insight / understanding**
— **Creating value**

The evolution of the list in response to what was happening in my life was significant. It confirms that it's important to evaluate what really matters to you on a fairly regular basis, so you can adjust your purpose — and thus what your energy should be focused on — to make sure it is still delivering meaning and fulfilment.

Your values map is a working document and will need updating regularly, as both your thinking evolves and your life experiences impact on its balance. It's worth keeping it somewhere accessible: a written list near your desktop, in your laptop bag, or by the bed. Somewhere you can regularly check on to see if the list is still current, and you are focusing your time and enthusiasm in the right places.

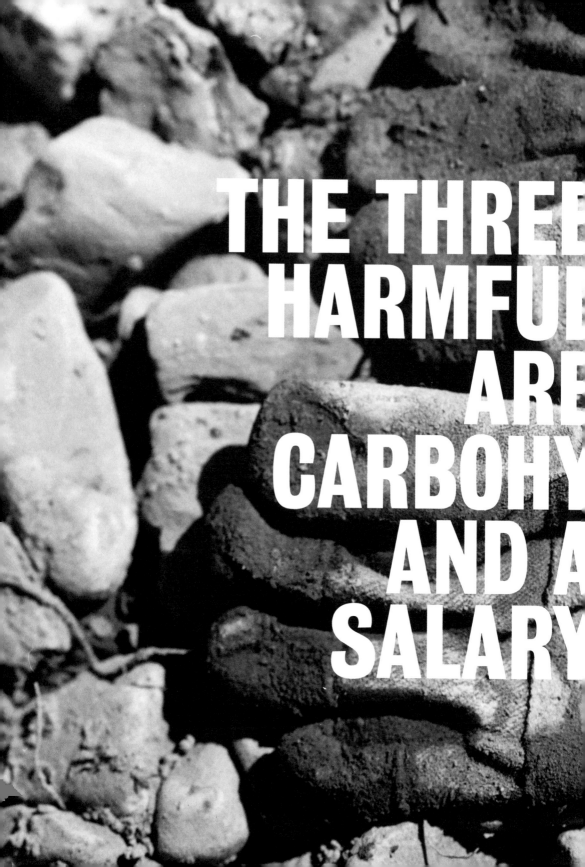

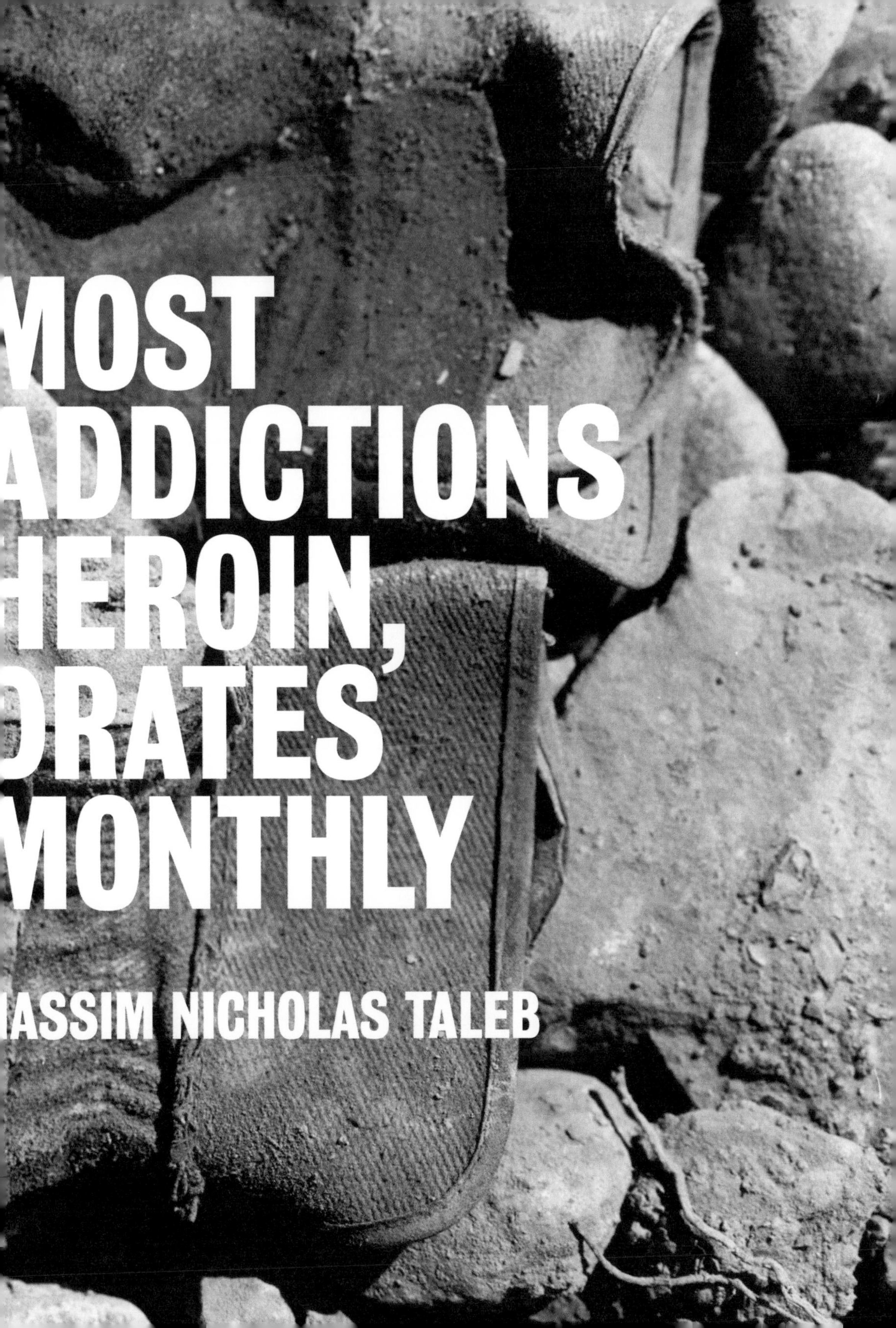

MOST
ADDICTIONS
HEROIN,
RATES'
MONTHLY

NASSIM NICHOLAS TALEB

# Confidence

This is it. This is the hummus in the sandwich. This is the main thing. Confidence is attractive. It is even 'sexy'. Getting closer to the real 'you' means you can stop projecting the fake one.

This section looks at confidence. It looks at why people struggle with confidence. How it varies from situation to situation. It examines and helps define limiting beliefs. It looks at who put them there. Why? How they can be inherited. How they are comfortable (like a pair of slippers), but how this doesn't serve anyone (like worn-out slippers). It looks at how to remove them.

Confidence is the key to a great talk. Confidence is not charisma (I can help teach confidence, but charisma is harder — it's more innate). Confidence is not ego (being good at something and knowing it is not having an ego; being average or poor at something and thinking you're great — that's ego). Confidence is not showing off — confidence is showing up, and showing up with belief in yourself and an understanding of your weaknesses as well as your strengths. It isn't bluffing or blagging or hustling. It is being utterly certain who you are.

Confidence is really complex. Some people seem to be born confident. There is interesting research suggesting that confidence is genetic — as much as 50 per cent of our likelihood of being confident is thought to be genetic. Some develop confidence (that'll be the other 50 per cent, then). Some have confidence knocked out of them (sometimes through love as much as hate) as they grow. But the good news is that there are many simple things you can do to improve confidence.

First, I want you to consider what confidence is. It isn't a fixed attribute. Sometimes we'll have more or less confidence in the same situation than at other times. Sometimes our confidence is dented by things that don't relate to the task in hand. Sometimes our confidence is bolstered (or undermined) by the clothes we choose to wear for an event.

Confidence is the outcome of the thoughts we have, the actions we take and how we feel about ourselves. Sure, these can all be affected by others, by external situations, by the journey to the event — or to this part of our lives. And fortunately, some of it can be rectified.

## Limiting beliefs

Before we get into the tips and tricks, the strategies and approaches, I want to talk about limiting beliefs. As I've mentioned, one of the things that holds us back in terms of confidence (and in so many other ways too) is our limiting beliefs. What is a limiting belief? It is a view of ourselves that keeps us small, that limits the person that we could be. It is a set view of ourselves that tightly defines us, that holds us down. This view has become normalised to the point that we can't even see the constraints on our own thinking. We have had these constraints for so long that they have become invisible. It's a bit like carrying around a big rucksack of pebbles. You become so used to the weight of the rucksack that you only notice the weight when you take the rucksack off. The rucksack has become part of you. It's the same with limiting beliefs, or fears. You only realise how constraining they were once they've gone. So how do we get rid of them?

There is a legendary experiment conducted by Karl Mobius, a German zoologist, in 1873 that demonstrates this beautifully. In the experiment Mobius placed a pike (a large carnivorous fish) in a big tank of water. Into the tank Mobius released a few smaller fish. As the pike was carnivorous, it ate the smaller fish. Mobius then lowered a large glass bell jar that was open at the bottom and the top into the tank. The pike was on the outside of the bell jar. Inside the jar Mobius placed more small fish. The pike could see the fish but not the glass bell jar. Eh up, it thought, dinner. It charged at the smaller fish and all it got in return was a sore nose. It tried to eat the smaller fish numerous times and just got more and more hurt and increasingly depressed. Finally, it seemed to give up. It sank to the bottom of the tank and looked glum. Mobius then lifted the bell jar out. There was now nothing between the pike and the smaller fish. Yet the pike stayed at the bottom of the tank. The smaller fish were free and swam all over the tank. Over the top of the pike, down its side and across its nose. Still the pike didn't budge. It didn't try and eat the smaller fish. Its limiting belief was that it couldn't. So it didn't even try.

Others repeated this experiment, in the days before animal cruelty was a thing. What do you think happened to the pike? Yep, that's right. It starved to death. Starved to death surrounded by food. We go bust surrounded by great business opportunities. We struggle to find the right people surrounded by the best talent in the world. We can't make ourselves heard but have every word at our beck and call. We run out of ideas surrounded by all the stimulus you could shake a stick at. Our limiting beliefs keep us where we are. We can't grow as a business because we don't do that 'thing', recruit those people, aren't brave enough to talk to those potential clients, deliver that presentation. We don't grow as people because our comfort zone is too damn comfortable. Because we can't express our ideas, our desires, our views, ourselves — we stay small. We stay safe. These are limiting beliefs and while they may have helped you in the past, may have helped you stay safe, they now hold you back. Time to thank them, and discard them.

It is really common to pick up a few limiting beliefs as we go through life. Some of those are given to us by our parents (mostly to keep us safe, occasionally to ensure we don't make them feel like they weren't 'enough'); sometimes by our colleagues or bosses at work (this is nearly always a result of them not wanting to be out-performed by you, or their desire to control you; I've seen this often in my thirty years in business, even in those who, allegedly, specialise in building teams — all driven by fear).

It is also really common for someone to steal your voice. They do this by intimating that what you say isn't important. This could simply be by not listening to you or it could be more strongly expressed. Rubbishing what people say is really common both at work and at home. No one has the right to silence you. Your words matter and they deserve to be heard. In my workshops I see this again and again, and sadly it is more common that women have their words stolen by men, than the other way around.

We inherit the limiting beliefs of our parents. You may be scared of money because your parents are, you may fear social interaction because your parents do, you may keep yourself small because your parents did the same, you may fear being seen or heard because your parents did. As J. K. Rowling says in her Harvard Commencement speech:

**There is an expiry date on blaming your parents.**

Thank your parents for keeping you safe, then ditch those constraints and become the person you always wanted to be.

Your limiting beliefs have kept you in your comfort zone and they've done that really successfully, but they don't serve you any more. It's time to move on.

# YOUR TIME IS LIMITED. REMEMBER THAT.

Each day you're given 86,400 seconds from the 'Time Bank'. Everyone is given the same. There are no exceptions. Once you make your withdrawal, you're free to spend it as you want.

The 'Time Bank' won't tell you how to spend it. Time poorly spent will not be replaced with more time. Time doesn't do refunds.

Time is your biggest gift. Indeed, it is more valuable than money as you can make more money, but not more time. But there is one simple truth: Your time is limited. And one day you will go to the bank and it won't have any more for you. And it will be at that exact moment that you will know the answer to these simple questions:

Did I use my time well?

Did I do what mattered most to me?

Did I find my love?

And did I pursue it like a wild hungry dog?

# Time to pause

Time, they say, is a scarce commodity. Underlying this idea is the morbid but unavoidable truth that, one day, we all die. A common response to this is to try and cram in as much as possible while we are here. This is understandable and often unconscious. It is particularly strong in the modern, industrialised West, where the feeling of time scarcity, coupled with the Protestant work ethic, contributes to the popularity of life hacks and productivity tips.

Yet there is more to life than getting things done. Time isn't a commodity at all, scarce or otherwise; it isn't a uniform, undifferentiated, raw material (even to a physicist, there is more to time than that). Time, as we experience it, is wildly different, depending on what we are doing. A minute waiting for the bus is not the same as a minute doing press-ups or a minute savouring the taste of ice cream. A year at work is not comparable to a year spent travelling. We may have a limited amount of time available to us in this life, as measured by the clock, but you are not a clock.

I want to invite you to let go of the idea that time is linear, regular and objective, and think of it in the same way we experience it — as elastic, variable and layered. I am not so interested in how you cram more into your life, but in how you get more out. To do so may require all sorts of strategies, but one thing I am sure of: it entails being able to pause.

A pause is an opening. It acts as a portal to other options and choices, giving more dimension to your experience. Just as a small amount of yeast makes heavy dough light, a small amount of pause here and there can leaven or lighten your life. You don't need much but it is a vital ingredient.

A book is a medium that lends itself to pausing — you get to choose when to dwell on something, when to re-read a sentence, or when to put the book down, which is one of the joys of reading. So while you will find lots of ideas about pausing in this book, you don't need to wait until you have finished it; you could stop reading right here, right now ... and pause. You might ask yourself why you were drawn to this book, and take a few moments to contemplate what it is that attracted you. Or you might take that moment to enjoy the view, or notice how you feel, or let your mind wander. The book will still be here for you later, to pick up again whenever you wish.

Experimenting with pause gives you a way to play around with the rhythms of your life. It gives you a way to give shape and texture to your experience, weakening the sensation that your life is driven by external forces over which you have no influence. Choosing where you put your pauses makes an enormous difference to what your life feels like and what you can do as a result.

You might pause to rest and regenerate, to become more creative, to connect with other people or yourself, or just to enjoy whatever it is that is going on around you (or inside you). There are many possible reasons to pause, ways to pause and lengths of pause. There are many different practices you can adopt. You can play around to your heart's desire and choose whatever suits you: pause is quite the opposite of a task to tick off. Pause is a very plastic concept. There is plenty to try. It is a subtle, powerful, life-giving idea — one that is worth spending a little time with.

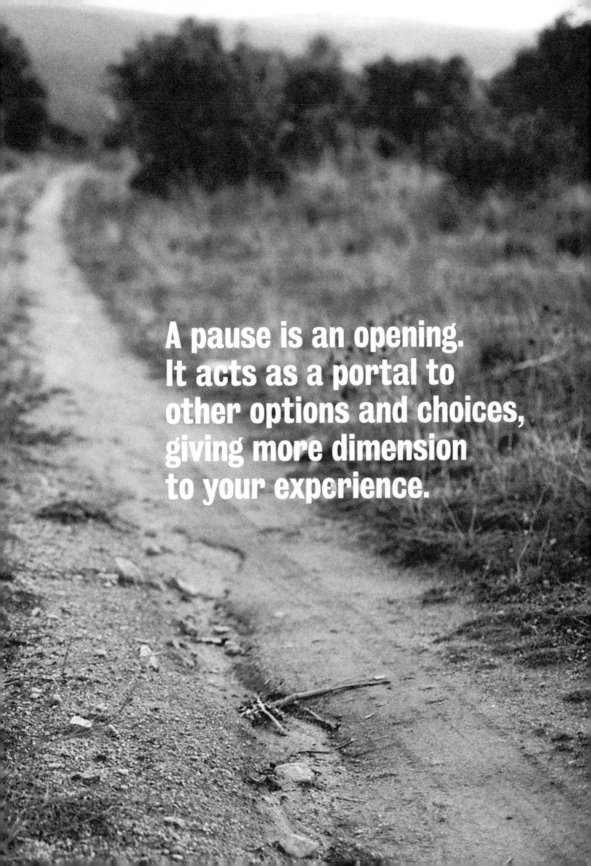

A pause is an opening. It acts as a portal to other options and choices, giving more dimension to your experience.

# Making time

**Time is the most valuable thing a man can spend.**

— Theophrastus

Time's a slippery snake — when you need more, it goes faster, when you want to speed things up a notch, it seems to slow right down. I would love to let you in on the secret to controlling time, but we all know it doesn't exist.

The reality, however, is exciting and liberating. You have the same 24 hours as everyone else. On the surface, that sounds depressing, right? 'OK, we all have the same amount of hours in a day to try and get everything done.' Well, yeah, you could think of it that way. Another way I like to think of it is:

**I have the same amount of time to create as Mozart did!**

Or:

**Me and Marie Curie are time buddies!**

The point is, everyone else in history — our heroes, the people we look up to and admire — had the same time constraints as us. And at some point they will have said, 'Oh I say, there are just not enough hours in the day!'

No one has the time — you have to make the time. These people have gone on to make things, do things, create things that changed the world. Yes, yes, yes, I know that's because they're immensely talented, but creation isn't just about talent — that's only half of it — you've got to do the work. You can be the smartest cat in the room, but if you choose to sit on the sofa eating Wotsits all day, nothing's gonna get done!

Here's the other thing. It's not about working more hours, it's about being smarter with your time. We have to be clever about what we spend our time on. For me, it's about spreading it between all my passions: family, friends, work, play, personal projects, wellbeing. That's why it's tricky. If it was purely about putting the hours in then that'd be easy, I'd tell you to work for 23 hours a day and sleep for one. But that's bonkers and definitely not the answer. It's a delicate balancing act that's personal to you and your situation. You have to decide when, where and how you'll spend those precious ticks and tocks.

## Finding the balance

Much like finding the time, I'm afraid that finding the balance is really difficult! That's because it's different for everyone. It's like alchemy: a magical and mystical combination of ingredients to achieve the perfect recipe for a harmonious life. It will pay to find more balance, because you'll find yourself more productive, healthier and happier if you can find the groove that works for you.

What's more, your balance will be ever shifting. You need to constantly review what you're doing and how you're feeling, to see what's working for you. The good news is, it gets easier the more you do it. You'll notice patterns of when you're grumpy and tired (because you start asking yourself, 'Why am I grumpy and tired?') and once you start to identify your own patterns, you can rectify them much more easily and quickly.

'Why are you banging on about balance though?' I can hear you scream, albeit quietly and calmly. Well, because I don't think the attitude 'Work more hours than anyone else' is right, or enough to really succeed and be happy. What you achieve in 18 hours might only have the same value as someone that's beavered away for three hours. It isn't about volume, it's about substance, and you can only give your best to something when your body and brain are satisfied.

You need to be a human being, to experience the world around you, with people around you. It'll make you a better 'DOer', I promise!

# Be patient

It is only recently that I have realised I cannot always fix things by quick action. Sometimes other work or lack of time has resulted in not managing to get round to every single job I had planned. This winter I left my garden beds messy and uncleared. The old plants were battered by frost and weather until the skeletons of summer fell on the earth. They became a natural mulch, offering the soil some defence against the elements. Clover self-seeded and covered many of the beds. I whipped out the occasional stray weeds but that was all.

Our culture leans towards the idea that we should intervene and that our results should be visible. To manipulate and control without really questioning why we are doing what we do. Much of the time I have found you only need to fix things if they have been put out of kilter in the first place.

I first heard about 'no dig' gardening from Charles Dowding, who has been pioneering and trialling this method since the year I was born. On its publication, I immediately bought his book *Organic Gardening: The Natural No-Dig Way* and have since become an absolute fan. In the book he argues that digging — though very occasionally necessary to get rid of weeds or a green manure — damages the soil and is often an unnecessary toil. Instead add compost and let the worms take it down and dig for you. Worms will do a much gentler job. Sometimes less is more.

Words from *Do Grow* by Alice Holden

# Time is earthed

The garden that I have been tending for the last two decades is magnificent. In the summer when the sun is up and the wind calm, it is its own timeless paradise.

Down one side is a long beech hedge, several metres high. Twenty years ago there were just twigs in the ground struggling to survive for lack of water. For a whole summer I relentlessly carried pails of water to quench the thirst of these young plants. We had no hosepipe that could reach to the end of the garden.

Over a few years some of the beech died, leaving big gaps. Standing one day with my father-in-law, I suggested we buy replacements the same height as the existing hedge. My logic: speed, ease, money. No problem. He gave me an old-fashioned look. Narrowing his eyes, he sighed and shook his head, saying, 'It's the roots you need to be concerned about. Not its height. If you want a beautiful hedge, invest in good roots, don't go for a quick fix. Your way would mean most of the plants you bought would die.'

So we bought small plants with strong roots. Today it is a magnificent hedge — bronzed for the autumn and winter months, deep lush green for spring and summer. Some things can take the time they need. Not the time you think they need. Time, like the hedge, is earthed.

# The ballad of Willie Nelson

If you believe that our best work is done when we are young, you create a grey future. Every day is the opportunity for the new, as yesterday has now gone. Drawing from a bitter well is not good for creativity.

Willie Nelson has made 250 albums, and is still touring in his eighties. He did not get a break until he was 40.

The author Mary Wesley was not published until she was 70 — she ended up being one of Britain's most successful novelists, selling 3 million copies of her books, including 10 bestsellers in the last 20 years of her life.

You can beat yourself up about not getting there soon enough, believing opportunity has passed you by. If that is what you believe, it is true.

Or you can believe that when success arrives it is the right time, and all before has been your preparation.

# A bit about me

by Lucy Gannon

Let me tell you about how I arrived in the world of television.
I had never considered becoming a writer. I was 39 and we were
living on a large council estate in Derby where I was working in
a home for adults with learning difficulties. My husband was an
engineer, designing sugar refineries, but his industry had shrunk
and he was out of work, so I was the breadwinner (and there wasn't
a lot of bread to be had on my wages). I'd left school at 16 and
never excelled at anything much but my life had been full of event
and travel, mountain tops and dark valleys, bereavements and
adventures. We had been to the theatre just once, when we were
given free tickets, and it was OK but not good enough to make us
return. We were ordinary people, as far away from writing, drama
and the theatrical world as anyone ever could be.

And then I heard about a competition in the *Radio Times* —
the Richard Burton Drama Award — write a play and win £2,000!
It was 1986 and that was a whole lot of money. Because we were
broke, I had been entering a lot of competitions, collecting tops
from Fairy Liquid bottles for one, saving coupons for free spot-the-
ball entries for another. Write a play? That was a new idea. I didn't
have the foggiest idea how to get started, so I found a couple of
published plays in the library to see how they were set out and
I borrowed a portable typewriter and scrounged up some paper.
But what could I write about?

I remembered a young man I had, silently, called Tom. I had never met Tom but once a month we went from Derby to visit my father in Norfolk. On the way there was a raised section of road, a bypass curving around a village. Down below us was a small bungalow, and that was where I had seen the man I secretly called Tom. My Tom was obviously physically and mentally disabled, and I would sometimes see him sitting in the patio windows of that tiny house, in a high-backed chair, a table attached to the front of it — a familiar sight to me, working as I did with disabled adults. I had wondered, over the months, about life in that tiny bungalow, caring for such a big, strapping young man who was so dependent. I thought about the love and the commitment, the sheer hard slog, the pain and the quiet rewards of those lives. And that's what I wrote my play about.

I was working 24-hour shifts in the care home, starting at lunch time one day, working through until 10pm and then staying there in the 'sleep-in' room, to be on hand for the night staff if they needed help. I started taking my typewriter along so that I could write in the quiet of the night. What an amazing revelation it was when I started writing! I had a voice! No sooner had I started than I was hooked. The other staff would hear me hammering away (two-finger plonking then — and still) and would bring me coffee through the night, until I admitted defeat and crawled into bed at three or four o'clock. The excitement of those nights was electric! I would wake up desperate to get back to the script for the next scene, the next piece of dialogue. It didn't quite write itself but there were times when I felt as if I didn't have much to do with the imagined world spilling out of me, vibrant and intriguing.

I didn't know if it was good or rubbish or somewhere in between, and I didn't really care! I was in a fever. No sooner was *Keeping Tom Nice* finished and posted off to the competition than I began my second, *Wicked Old Nellie*. But I still had no idea if what I was doing would mean anything at all to anyone else. What was I to do with the second play when it was finished? Who could I send this one to?

There was a theatre in Derby, so I dropped it off at the stage door, went home and started my third play, *Raping the Gold*.

I was maybe two scenes into this third play when I had a call from the BBC to say that *Keeping Tom Nice* was on the shortlist for the awards.

My play won the award and it was taken on tour by the Royal Shakespeare Company. Directors from the Bush Theatre read the script and commissioned me to write *Raping the Gold*, and the director of Derby Playhouse, Annie Castledine, finally got around to looking at *Wicked Old Nellie* — and began the production process there. Suddenly I was in the world of theatre, but I still hadn't managed to see anything on the stage. Sally Burton, Richard's widow, encouraged me to take up my residency with the RSC (part of the award) and paid my wages for six months so that I could afford to stay at home and write. And I finally went to see a play. Unfortunately, it was *Titus Andronicus*, Shakespeare's most violent offering (and, I later learned, a particularly gruesome production). There I was, a middle-aged care worker from Derby, watching rape, child slaughter, mutilation, beheading and cannibalism on what I had thought would be a 'nice evening out'. I drove back to Derby, shell-shocked, and as I clambered into bed next to my snoozing husband he murmured, 'How was it?' And I answered, 'Bloody horrible.'

So how, after that naive beginning, did I morph from theatre into TV, and why? It had very little to do with me! In the audience of *Raping the Gold*, at the tiny Bush Theatre, a script editor from ITV, an independent film producer and a producer from the BBC all liked the writing and ended up commissioning me.

Suddenly, I was in TV. Up to my neck in television. But it all started with a borrowed typewriter and a sense of 'have a go'. There is no golden path into television or film. But the world is hungry, ravenous, desperate for talent. You are the talent. If you write, they will find you. But they will not find you until you write.

We are all born with abilities and talents. Some of us discover what they are before it's too late. That's a blessing. You may be hesitant and even apologetic about your desire to write, maybe asking yourself, 'Am I talented?' And if that's what you're wondering right now, you are not alone. When creative people meet, the question often veers around to 'What is talent?' I've bumbled around this question with painters, writers, sculptors, poets, potters and musicians. There is no definitive answer because talent can't be seen or tasted or measured, and what sounds beautiful to one listener is flat and uninteresting to another. The words that excite you may leave me cold, and we are all, in our deepest appreciation of the world around us, biased. Our bias is created not by reasoning and decision-making, but by the unique chemistry of our personality, our past, our environment, our ethics and the reactions we create in others.

Here is my understanding, simply the conclusion I've come to so far, and the phrases I've found that — in part, anyway — help me to find an understanding of talent:

**Talent is generosity of spirit.**

**Talent is the human spirit reaching out, hungry
to connect, to understand and to be understood,
to shed pretence and reveal the truth of who we are.
To look beyond the visible and tangible to the eternal.
Talent is vulnerable. It demands that the artist, writer,
musician invites rejection with everything they do.
Talent is that struggle to put potatoes on the table
not by ploughing but by dreaming. Talent is not an
easy lover. It's a bugger to live with. It's demanding,
relentless and exhausting. But it's precious and the
greatest gift of all. It's passion.**

Words from *Do Drama* by Lucy Gannon    51

# Conscious living

**As you get older, the questions come down to about two or three. How long? And what do I do with the time I've got left?**

— David Bowie

Buddhists talk about the concept of experiencing each night as a small death and waking up to a new reality the next morning. They view the new day as a chance to do things differently and to let go of anything that doesn't serve them.

Conscious living is about waking up to how you live, being aware of your remaining time and living it passionately and mindfully, and connecting with yourself and others. It doesn't mean being the most successful or the wealthiest but rather having a meaningful life doing what matters to you, and being who you want to be.

## Life review

Part of accepting death when you are dying is accepting the life you've had in order to let go of it more easily. The big question is, was it a good one?

I met a lovely lady who was in the last few weeks of her life. She was in her mid-sixties. Her husband told me about the plans they'd had to go travelling and to live in the countryside after she retired. She became ill not long after retiring and her health rapidly deteriorated. They never got to accomplish any of their plans. Often people wait until they retire to do something they love. Do it today, not in years to come. Don't procrastinate!

One exercise you could do now is to write your own 'living obituary'. What's your life story to date? Do this chronologically from birth to the present. You can mark significant events — positive and negative — qualities, relationships and other influential people. What would you say about your life so far? It might prompt you to think about some of the following:

— **What am I proud of?**

— **Does my life have meaning and purpose?**

— **Am I content?**

— **Am I doing what matters to me?**

— **Do I spend quality time with and appreciate those I love?**

— **Am I the person I want to be?**

— **Do I live a life for myself or what others expect of me?**

— **What can I learn?**

— **Am I using my time wisely?**

— **Do I help others?**

— **Am I a giver?**

You are the maker of your own story. If you want to rewrite it, be conscious of your thoughts. How do they make you feel? If you tell yourself you can't do something then that's what you'll believe. If you want to make changes in your life, to live better, allow yourself to be brave, think about a new reality, then do one small thing every day to create it. What will your remaining story be?

# Chronos and Kairos

It's tempting to put change off. To leave it until later. I coach people in business and I hear this a lot: 'When I retire I'm going to give something back/do the thing I always dreamt of.' I call this life-offset. It goes something like this: You spend 40 years doing something you don't love so that you can spend five years doing something you've always wanted to do. My advice is to reverse it.

But sometimes it's hard to work out what you want to do. We all have a feeling that there's something waiting for us. It's frustrating to watch time tick past. But remember that there are two types of time: Chronos and Kairos. Chronos is one of the Greek concepts of time. It refers to the linear, measurable flow of seconds, minutes, hours, days, weeks, months and years. My mate Dave brought Chronos into sharp focus this summer. I remarked how great the summer was. 'Enjoy it, you've probably only got another 40,' he said. Yep, I thought, and I'll be incontinent for the last 10. This is the trap of Chronos time: it feels like it is running out.

Think instead about the other Greek definition of time: Kairos. Kairos means the right or opportune moment. You may have run out of Chronos time but have loads of perfect moments left. Sometimes the time is right for things and sometimes it isn't. But you can start thinking about stuff now. In fact there is only one time to begin thinking and that is...

NOW

As Jessie J said, 'It's not about the money.'

If you were solely interested in money you wouldn't be reading this. Money is important. We all need to live and we all need to earn. But earning it the right way is important.

Mickey Smith (a Do Lectures speaker from 2011) says in his film *Dark Side of the Lens*:

# 'IF I CAN ONLY SCRAPE A LIVING, AT LEAST IT WILL BE A LIVING WORTH SCRAPING.'

These words haunt me. This sense of worth, of purpose, of value is missing from many lives. Time to change that.

Of course you may not want to change the world. That may not be your bag. And that's cool (but it's getting warmer).

It might be that you're just bored doing what you do.

So you need to change it.

# Here's a little exercise to underline why.

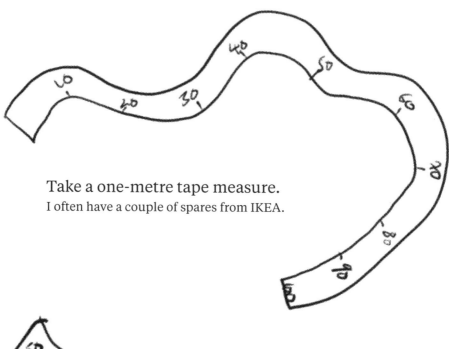

Take a one-metre tape measure.
I often have a couple of spares from IKEA.

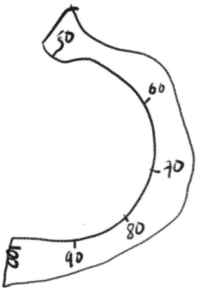

Cut it at your age — for me it's 48.

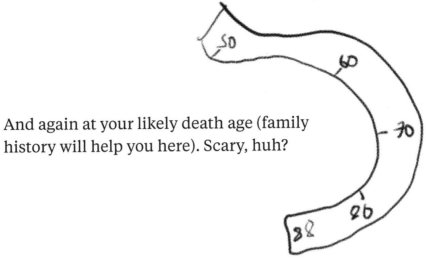

And again at your likely death age (family history will help you here). Scary, huh?

And again at when you expect to retire.*

**So that's what I've got left.**
And I'll spend a third of this time sleeping. Better get cracking then.

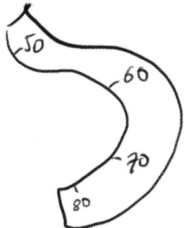

# YOU'LL ONLY REGRET THE THINGS THAT YOU DON'T DO.

\* I've got four kids, I may never retire.

# Be open to change

Change can mean different things to different people. It can be exciting, terrifying, something to be feared or to be embraced. But the truth is we all need to be open to the idea of change.

To move forwards something usually has to change. It could be as simple as swapping what kind of pencil you use or as profound as altering your whole belief system. No matter what the scale of change is, they're all valid, as it means you're starting to consider other possibilities or other ways of doing things.

Sometimes the hardest part can be realising and then accepting that things need to change. It's hard because it's scary. Really scary. Having comfort in our routine is lovely. It's… it's… comfortable, and that's a lovely feeling. To suddenly disrupt that feels bonkers, but sometimes it has to be done in order to get to a better place. Think of it as a bit of turbulence. Trust me, it'll soon pass and then you'll be above the clouds!

So, you want to change things? You want something new? Good. Good! If you're in a rut, I'm not going to help you get out. I'm going to show you how to get out of it yourself.

# Be the change you want to see

Obviously this chapter is being super-idealistic and all these nice floaty sentiments about just doing what you love, blah, blah, are annoying, right? Well, maybe I am an idealist. But why wouldn't you want to try to create your ideal world to live in?

It's so easy to get eaten up with cynicism and negativity, thinking that the good stuff doesn't happen to people like you, and the opportunities just don't present themselves. So start by redirecting some of your time and energy to change that. Start bridging gaps, start conversations, start sowing seeds. Don't focus on what isn't happening, focus on what could happen.

If you don't feel there's a group that represents you — start it. If there's something missing from the conversation — introduce it. If you're working within a larger organisation you'll have to find the boundaries of what you can and can't change. Push gently against the things you'd like to be different, help and encourage others with things you'd like to see change. I'm not advocating a hostile or aggressive position, totally the opposite — you can make changes by being a kind, warm and passionate person.

My friend and fellow speaker at the Do Lectures, Sarah Corbett, founded the 'Craftivist Collective', which combines craft (usually in the form of cross-stitching) and activism to engage people in social change. She does this respectfully and peacefully as 'gentle activism'. And it works. A few years ago, Sarah was constantly pestering her local MP — sending petitions and forwarding on issues — so much so that the MP told her to stop, saying, 'It's a waste of your time and my time.' Obviously frustrated with such a response, Sarah knew she had to appeal to the MP in a different way, so she decided to provoke rather than preach. She used her craft skills to make the MP a handkerchief, embroidered with a personal message and the line, 'Don't blow it!'

This personal touch led to Sarah meeting with the MP; they sat down and talked with each other, rather than at each other.

It's proof that to make changes you don't have to be an extrovert or a lunatic, you just have to have drive and purpose. How you manifest that drive is up to you — there's no right or wrong way.

And things will naturally change too. So you'll have to constantly re-evaluate yourself. What you want and need from your work and personal life can and will change often. So be sure to take time out every now and then to take stock of what you're thinking and feeling.

In practical terms, you can do that by just stepping outside of your normal routine — disrupt your schedule a little and give yourself a bit of time to reflect. Make a mental note to check in with yourself regularly. It could be as grand as scheduling a mini-holiday to take some time out and assess your life and work. Try and go away on your own — radical, eh? Or it could be as simple as using a train journey to switch off the social media and just contemplate. Are you happy? Are you being the change you want to see? Ask yourself these questions.

As much as this is an individual pursuit, do take a look at what other people need too. Do your ideas and goals line up with what your colleagues and comrades are doing? Do you believe there's a better way to do something that will benefit everyone? Collaborating with others to make change happen can bring it about much quicker, so seek out those positive souls who share your desire for change.

Communication is also key for those who don't want change. In an organisation of any shape or size there will be opposition, so being able to passionately relay your desire for making things different is essential. Sarah's Craftivist manifesto point, 'Provoke Don't Preach', fits perfectly with this — encourage discussion and new points of view, don't force it. Force is often met with resistance.

Change? It's suddenly sounding like a long tightrope to walk, isn't it? It sure as hell won't be easy but it'll be worth it. You want to get to the other side, right?

NEW

DESTINATION

CHAP SEC PG
00-01-09

BE

HPPY

CHAP SEC PG
02-03-28

SAY

YES

CHAP SEC PG
03-02-40

MAKE

TIME

CHAP SEC PG
05-03-84

BE THE

SUN

04-03-71

GRFT

AND CRFT

06-01-106  CHAP SEC PG

CHAP SEC PG
03-04-44

TEACH

YOURSELF

BE THE

CHNGE

CHAP SEC PG
02·01·23

FIND

BLNCE

CHAP SEC PG
05-04-86

# PEOPLE WHO SAY IT CANNOT BE DONE SHOULD NOT INTERRUPT THOSE WHO ARE DOING IT.

— George Bernard Shaw

# Turn the internet off

Treat distractions as the enemy. Luckily, each electrical device you have comes with an off button. Remember, your time is limited. But your ability to be distracted is infinite. If you want to get things done, you have to focus. And focus comes from blocking out that busy world out there.

I am not good at email. But I am good at getting things done. I view email as a distraction from making things happen. I view getting things done as more important than having an empty inbox. I have bought all the apps to help me cope with email. But they don't work for me. It's not them. It's me.

The internet is brilliant but it is one very efficient way of using your time. It's a super-addictive distraction device that will stop us from getting stuff done if we allow it to.

Just click the off button. You've got things to do.

# One-nighters and self-imposed deadlines

Sometimes getting started is just as difficult as finishing something. You have every reason in the world to put it off: 'I don't have time to dedicate to it', 'It's not the right time', 'I don't have the money needed right now', 'I'm tired', 'Bake Off is on telly'.

There are always plenty of reasons for not starting a new project or venture, and some of them are valid and some of them aren't. But the thing is, it is hard starting something new. It does take a lot of energy and willpower, which is precious and hard to come by. That's why I like to do little bitesize chunks of 'new'.

I call them 'one-nighters' and it's where I indulge myself in a new micro-project but only give myself one evening.

The end result is normally a silly little video or a poster for a fictional band, but I get something out of it! Now, I'm talking in design terms, as that's what I do, but it doesn't have to be at all. You could write a short story. Compose a 15-second opera. Organise a coffee morning. Try out a new recipe. Whatever it is, you get something out of it.

Think of it as training. In order to get fit you have to exercise. Small bursts of exertion to build up the muscle mass to get fitter and stronger. You can't run a marathon without doing a few 5ks first, so get those little-and-often training exercises under your belt and you'll soon find yourself flying past your competitors.

# WORK EACH DAY
# TOWARDS THE GOAL
**(obsession ... ahh, the smell of it)**

# 99% OF BUSINESSES FAIL FOR ONE REASON

They don't start. The start line is the scariest place. Step beyond it and you can be judged. Step beyond it and you can fail. Step beyond it and you can no longer hide behind what might have been.

Most people talk about starting something one day. But 'one day' doesn't ever come along. They don't get past the start line. Their ideas are probably good enough to succeed. But their belief isn't strong enough.

The patent office doesn't hold the best ideas. They sit in the back of your head waiting for you to believe in them enough to start.

Once you pass that line, you are in the 1% club. Those rare people who turn their ideas into real things. Boom.

# BEGIN BEFORE
# YOU ARE READY

There's a point on a runway during take-off that a plane reaches V1 speed. Once it passes V1, it has reached the point of no return. It has to take off. Or crash. In order to determine its V1 speed every plane will factor in its weight, wind-speed, weather conditions, slope, length of runway, etc. So although there's not a physical line drawn on each runway, it's there.

But when it comes to starting a business, for example, there's no calculation to tell us when the right time is.

So what happens? We defer. We put barriers up to justify not starting. 'The economy isn't great.' 'I've got a big mortgage.' 'I need more experience.' But as you put those barriers up, only you can tear them down.

There will never be a right time to start. Accept it. So start now.

PLEASE WATCH
YOUR HEAD
ON THE
SCAFFOLDING

# IDEAS

How we learn.
How we communicate.
What we eat.
How we play.
How we exercise.
Where we live.
How we travel.
Our behaviour.
Our governments.
Our corporations.
The music we listen to.
How we relax.
How we stay awake.
The status quo.
The perceived wisdom.
'This is how we do
things around here.'

IDEAS
CHANGE
EVERYTHING

# SO WHAT'S YOUR IDEA THEN ?

Maybe you've not got one yet. This exercise looks at what you love to do. If you already have an idea, stay with me for a bit longer, it won't hurt to go over this stuff. Opposite, you'll see three columns with titles:

— **Things you like doing**
— **Things you care about**
— **Things you are good at**

Spend some time filling them in. Be honest, you're defining your purpose here.

Things you are good at

Things you care about

Things you like doing

So you've listed your passions, your skills and the things that give you pleasure. Now I want you to spend a half-hour thinking about how these could all come together. Think about some crazy stuff and some boring stuff then list them below.

# MY BIG LIST OF POSSIBLE IDEAS

Was that OK? Too difficult? A bit forced? That's ok.
This next exercise might help. Follow the steps through and you will end up with at least four possible ideas.

# IDEA GENERATOR

**5 – Four reasons this will work**

**4 – Twelve ways it might work**

1

2

3

4

5

6

7

8

9

10

11

12

For example: Would it be better if you added something to it?
Would it be better if you took something away? Would competitors
be scared? Why wouldn't people buy it? Is it physically possible?
Is it financially viable? Is it ownable? Is it simple?

**1 – What do you want to do?**
Rephrase it three times

**2 – How are you going to do it?**
Rephrase it three times

**3 – Four ways it won't work**

IDEAS

# Don't worry about being original, be honest

This is a bold statement, I know, but stick with me. Firstly, if you do have the power to be a true original, a true visionary, then well done you. You can skip this part!

If, like me, you're among the 99.9 per cent who aren't world-leading visionaries right out the gate, then this part is for you. Much like worrying about what other people's lives are like, you can't spend your energy or time worrying about doing something no one has done before. Because, dude, that's really, really hard.

Instead, concentrate on making and doing things you believe in. Do things that you love and can pour your heart into. Build on what others have built, but do it honestly. You never know, you might just honestly stumble across something totally original.

As an individual, you are unique. Your upbringing, your outlook, your loves, your hates, your passions, your fears — all that gets melted down into a sticky goo of creative lava and what solidifies out of that primordial ooze is totally unique to you.

That's why there's no point getting hung up on comparison. It's something you can't ever avoid, so just expect it will happen and carry on past it. It can be crippling when someone says, 'Oh yeah, I've seen that, it's just like X' — even though you've never heard of X. Don't let that stop you, put it to the back of your mind and carry on regardless. A Bristol friend called Miles once told me, 'Don't make it perfect, make it now.' I've never forgotten that.

# Some ideas are right in front of you

Dietrich Mateschitz went on holiday to Thailand and spotted lots of people drinking a native drink called Krating Daeng. He kept asking himself: 'What does that mean?' His radar was on. He didn't invent Red Bull. It already existed. He just took something he saw on holiday and turned it into a whole new category.

James Dyson wasn't the only person to walk past a sawmill and see the extractor fan at the top. The answer was available to anyone who asked the right question. But he was the only one to go and make vacuum cleaners using that technology. Yes, it took him five years and over 5,000 iterations. He didn't invent the idea. He took an idea from another industry and applied it to vacuum cleaners. He made it work.

A lot of times the ideas are there right in front of you just waiting for you to take that idea and put it into another industry or country.

# Ideas work like Velcro

Velcro works like this: On one side is a series of hooks going in lots of random directions. On the other side is a series of loops going in lots of random directions. When a hook meets a loop, they connect. It is in the connection business.

It is the randomness of the hooks and the loops that make Velcro work, but they are also important to us if we want to be interesting. We need to have lots of random hooks and loops. If we read the same old books, we get to know more about the thing we know lots about already. We need to subscribe to magazines that we wouldn't normally subscribe to; we need to go to places that we wouldn't normally go to, eat at places that may not be our kind of place.

We stay interesting by stepping outside our groove. We keep pushing; we leave what we know behind for a bit.

This is important from the point of view of coming up with ideas. If your reference points are different from other people's, then guess what, your ideas are going to be different. To think different: do different, read different, travel different, eat different, etc.

Velcro goes in many different directions in order to make a connection. If we are interested in new ideas, so should we.

# Some ideas are born ugly

Great ideas often have no reference points. We have nothing to compare them to. They are original, and awkward. And so they are the most vulnerable to people trying to kill them. They do not conform to what exists, so they challenge us.

So in order to keep the idea alive you will have to rely on your gut instinct, which sometimes is the hardest sell of all. You have to believe in it when no one else does. The parent has to love the ugly duckling until it turns into a little beauty.

We also judge ideas too quickly. It's not always clear from the beginning which are the good, the bad and the ugly. Learn not to judge them too quickly. That dumb idea could be the one. If you think conventionally you may dismiss the ugly duckling.

# 23 QUESTIONS TO ASK OF YOUR IDEA

IDEAS

1    **Is it a good idea?**

2    **Is it a new idea?**

3    **Is it scalable?**

4    **Will people want it?**

5    **What change will it bring about?**

6    **Is it investable?**

7    **Does it matter to you?**

8    **Does it matter to your customer?**

9    **How do you know?**

10    **How big is the change it can make?**

11    **Is it good for the planet?**

12    **Is it good for the human?**

13    **What is your niche?**

14    **How big is that niche?**

15    **How will you test it?**

16    **Does it solve a common problem?**

17    **Does this problem need solving?**

18    **What disruption will it bring?**

19    **Where will it be in five years' time?**

20    **Do you love it?**

21    **Would you spend ten years doing it?**

22    **What will its legacy be?**

23    **Uncertain about your idea now? Keep going.**

# Write your business plan on a doormat

When you order a doormat, they charge per word. This financial restriction makes you think long and hard about what you want to say. The other restriction is that space is limited.

So your thinking needs to be distilled down into the fewest number of words possible. So simple that it can appear on a doormat.

If you could apply the same discipline of writing a doormat to your business plan, I think the chances of you having plenty of customers walking on it would be increased. Why? Because you have no choice but to keep it simple and be clear. And simple and clear are good for business.

So ask yourself what it is that you want to stand for in the fewest number of words that you can:

Kickstarter: *Change funding of ideas.*
Patagonia: *Higher quality. Lower impact.*
Google: *Faster, more relevant search.*

The less you have to spend on the doormat, the more thinking you have done.

# Ideas need someone to make them happen

Ideas need doers, not talkers. Ideas require your total belief in them. So before you cross that line, just make sure you are 100 per cent into it. Businesses can fail for many reasons.

Perhaps the founders don't quite believe in the idea, or one of the partners loses his or her nerve when the first test comes at them.

A lack of belief can be much more damaging than a lack of funding. In football terms, this is the equivalent of not fully committing in the tackle. And when you are half-hearted in the tackle, you are much more likely to get injured.

Players who are saving themselves for the next big game or an important tournament often end up injured because they held back. Holding back often ends in tears.

Likewise, ideas need you to commit. They need all your money. They need all your time. They need all your energy. They need all your love. They need all your belief. If you are half-hearted about the idea, don't even start.

# SMALL BUDGETS
# REQUIRE BRAVE IDEAS

Great ideas cost no more than rubbish ones. That's nice to know. And, if you want to take the stress out of running a business, have a great idea.

Ideas don't care about who you are, where you are, they don't go to those with the most money or the biggest smile. They come to you in the bath, in the shower, while going for a run, when you least expect it, and when you need them most. But they will come to you. If you would only just listen. And that's a skill you need to learn.

Always be listening.

A great idea will get you more publicity, give you more energy, and will in the end give you more sales. Jake Burton invented a whole new sport: snowboarding. He didn't have a big budget. Just a big idea. A whole new sport.

# SANE PEOPLE QUIT

Starting a business is hard. You'll work like a crazy thing and have to sustain that over a long period of time. Poor pay. Terrible hours. Tons of stress. Any normal, rational person would quit. And that's what happens. When things get tough, and there will be a point when they do, sane people quit.

But purpose-driven entrepreneurs are different. They fall in love with the change they are making, so have to find a way to make it work. Their love stops them quitting. Love makes them persevere.

Love blinkers them to all the worry and stress. And it's their purpose that fuels that love.

IF YOU'RE
GOING TO TRY,
GO ALL THE WAY.
OTHERWISE,
DON'T EVEN START.

CHARLES BUKOWSKI

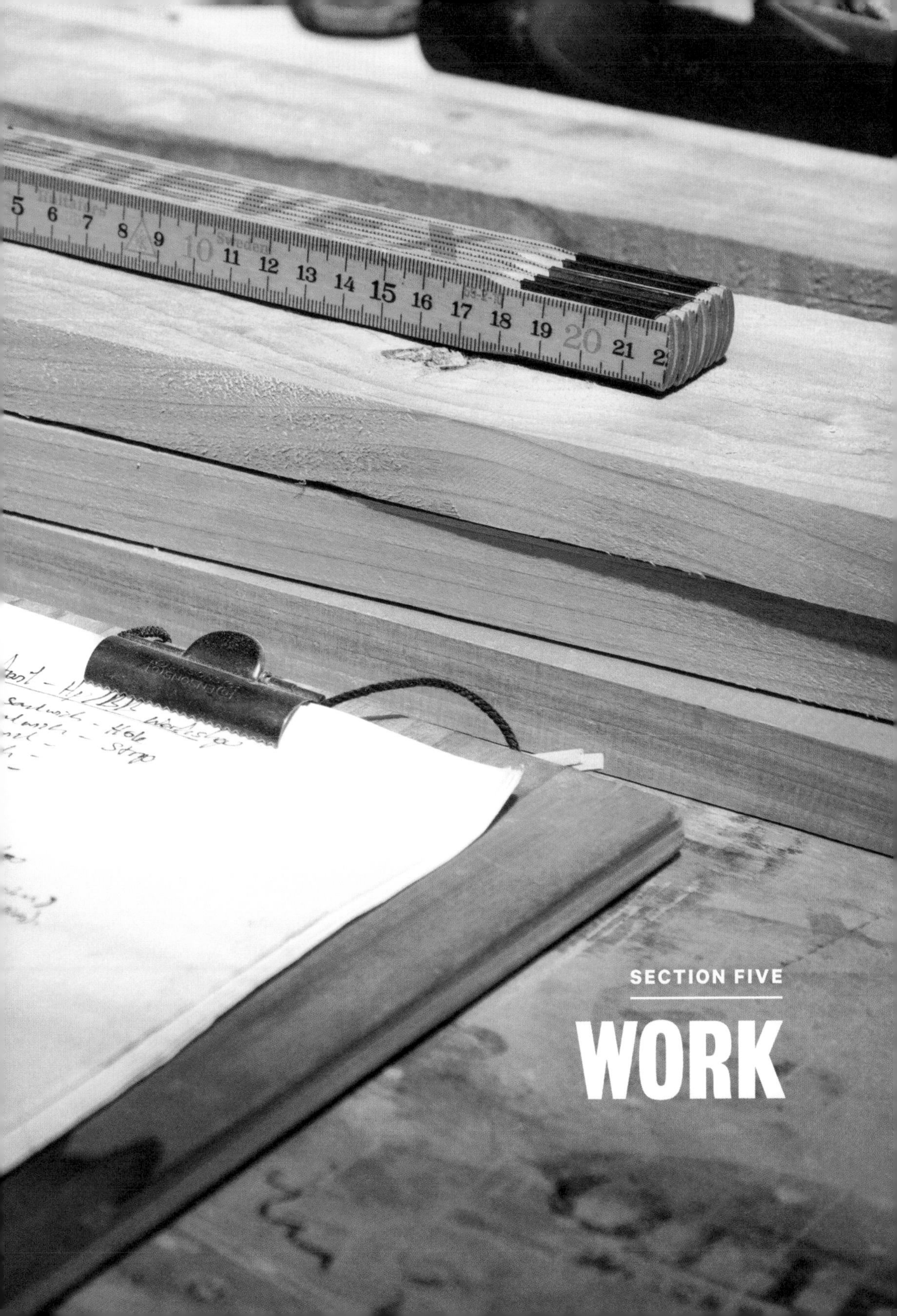

SECTION FIVE

# WORK

# RISE EARLY.
# WORK HARD.
# STRIKE OIL.

— John Paul Getty

Now we're on the runway, it's time to get down to business!

I want to kick things off by positively changing the way we look at 'work' because it should be something that excites us, not depresses us! While growing up, we can see work as the end of being childlike, the beginning of being an adult and a place where fun is strictly outlawed. I'm not sure where this comes from, as I don't think it has ever been said out loud. But it's certainly assumed.

This notion that work should be endured, that it is drudgery, is madness. It doesn't have to be! Now, there's a huge caveat here. There are loads of jobs out there that are laborious and downright difficult and I like to refer to that as 'real work'. And thank goodness there are some mighty fine people who are good at that stuff. So this section should really be called 'Work can be enjoyed, not endured'.

If, like me, you are lucky enough to work in a sector that requires creative thinking (and that's a massive scope of jobs) or want to get into the creative industries, then don't look at work as a necessity, think of it as an opportunity.

This might sound like I'm singling out the arts straight away and elevating it. But a 'creative' job isn't limited to artists, designers and those who colour in. No way. Creativity is used everywhere. It's problem solving — using knowledge, intuition and ingenuity to reach a desired outcome. So, that includes pretty much every kind of job ever then, right? Nice!

Ultimately, you need to adopt the right mindset. Try and put wages to one side for a minute. What if you look at work as a challenge, as a game, a way to level up? Most of us will spend a huge proportion of our lives working, so we should do something we enjoy, find interesting and engaging. It's an opportunity to change things, mould things, make things, break things and be downright disruptive.

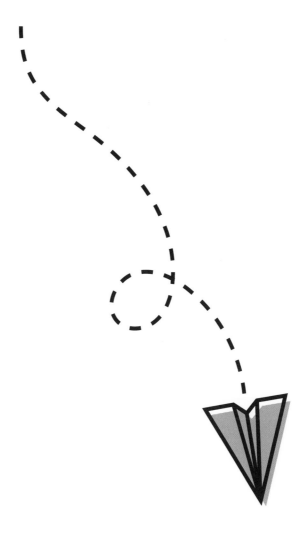

# Business can do good

**Before it is too late, we should embark in earnest on the most fundamental task facing modern civilisation, that of making any future growth compatible with the long-term preservation of the only biosphere we have.**

— Vaclav Smil

'What does the world need?' is one of the most pressing questions of our time. Why? Because this question encompasses a number of other questions: Why are we here? For what reason do we exist? What values create the foundation of what matters most? What kind of world are we trying to make? We must transform our mindset, but to what end?

The Coronavirus pandemic brought us to a moment of transformation at great speed. It was a tragedy but one that offered an extraordinary space for us to reimagine what a better future might look like for us all.

Now is the moment of opportunity. Business can do good. To remake our world, it can seek the good and manifest it in all that we create. If we are to build a future worth living in, we must try to achieve equilibrium between our economy, our environment and our community. And reimagine the role that business plays in their regeneration. That is what the world needs from business. That is what business needs to give the world.

We must turn away from the devastating effects of the quest for endless growth, pursuing profit at any and all cost. The universal virtue of doing good in business, combined with the need for a more life-changing and regenerative society, has been veiled for too long. We now stand on the edge: one third of the world's entire wealth is held in 'offshore' tax havens; we are beset by fires and floods; the glaciers are retreating from the mountains and calving themselves into the oceans at breakneck speed.

Your customers' needs have changed, too. For some time, a shift has been taking place in the discussion about what type of world we want to live in. This is fuelled by a generational shift in values, knowledge and understanding of how our world is not working for many people. Our children's generation has no ticket to the future. They won't have jobs for life. They won't have great returns on their pensions. Many of them know they won't ever be able to afford to buy a house. Yet, despite all of this, they are steeped in values. They think a lot about the environment and are deeply concerned with matters of social responsibility, equality and diversity.

Today, in business, there is a growing realisation that we are counting the wrong things, which diminishes how we see the world. We have lost the sense of life as a whole, as wholesome. We must start by accepting the interconnectedness of our natural world, because nature is not designed selfishly, but to serve and support the needs of all life. We need to measure success in a more nurturing and qualitative way. We need to ask: what is growth, what is progress and how do we measure these things?

We could start by appreciating the accomplishments of our economic growth over the last 200 years, but also acknowledging its increasing limitations. We must change the means by which we measure productivity, prosperity, sustainability, profit and loss, and review the business models designed for endless growth. We need to measure carbon capture, regeneration and quality of life. I want to show you how you can deliver the equilibrium that the world needs. I do not draw from the wishing well of 'make believe', but from the hard truth of people living in the real world, who demand positive and lasting change. They are ready to create, make and build that new reality. Perhaps it's only a matter of time before people go to Mars. But not everyone is going to Mars, so we might as well fix the planet we already have.

# Love the work you do:
# Blitz Motorcycles

Hugo and Fred build motorcycles. They build them from discarded older motorbikes, curating their builds using the frames, engines, petrol tanks and handlebars from machines of another time. They call their company Blitz — as in giving new life, new energy, new purpose, to old motorcycles.

Possessed with an aesthetic vision of how these motorcycles could be reclaimed, then reborn as something new and exciting to ride, Hugo and Fred laboured after their love. For them, motorcycles, and motorcycle mechanics, are a passion. The preservation of a time of motorcycle engineering became their quest. Kick-started from the place that makes the heart beat a little faster — the sound motorcycles make, the way they feel riding through Parisian streets or through the dusty back roads of another country — wherever they are, Blitz motorcycles speak to the soul. If the existentialist poet Thom Gunn was alive today his poetry would thrum to an engine hanging in the heat of a Blitz motorcycle and the leather-jacketed riders directing their trajectory forwards.

Hugo and Fred taught themselves about motorcycle mechanics, learning through trial and error. It took a little time, as it always does to become a master of your craft. They persevered, knowing that time is earthed. You can't rush to greatness, you can't guarantee it — you can only work towards it by practising your craft every day, directed by your passion, by your purpose.

Sacrifice can involve money, and time doing other things, but that all adds up to realising a purpose which gives much greater rewards. The reordering of happiness, work and play. Hugo and Fred speak of working joyfully together, they speak of the joy of continuously learning. Surely this is the true mark of the pursuit of craftsmanship, the revelation of beauty and its rewards. And they speak of taking an autonomous position, a place where one can live and work without debt and the many life challenges debt can create.

Simply, these machines take time to build, as each one is unique; there are no timesheets, only love as the arbiter of good work and a day's toil. Fred and Hugo say they have met more interesting people in the few years they have been working as Blitz than in the previous ten years: 'They are more interesting, because they have a passion like us.' They treasure every day.

Watch people who love what they do. Feel their passion. Listen to how they describe their work.

Investing in loving what you do always costs time, money and sometimes the odd scar and bruise. It repays that love with personal satisfaction, and in turn it inspires, guides and nurtures the spirit in others. If we invested in more things that give us a meaningful life, our world might feel a little different. And our work might even outlive us.

As a good friend said to me, 'Invest in love, it pays well in the end.'

# The art of doing

**Anxiety is caused by a lack of control, organisation, preparation and action.**

— David Kekich

No one teaches us the art of doing. We are thrown in the deep end at school, somehow avoid drowning in university or college and end up splashing wildly through our working lives. The emphasis is on results, not on how you get there. The solutions to our chaos are sold to us in the form of books, apps, filing systems and beautifully designed stationery and bespoke pens and pencils. And we consume them avidly. Alas, they offer only temporary respite. Because the only solution to us being disorganised is getting organised!

So if you are reluctantly accepting that it's you who might need to change, you are on the right track. And it's not only about doing more: by learning the art of doing you will also discover the art of being too. This section will take you through a simplified approach that I have implemented personally and coached many others in. It is not a complete guide but will give you enough to be getting on with.

## CARE about what you do

The simple framework that I use myself and with my coaching clients is to 'C-A-R-E' about what they do:

Collect ▷ Arrange ▷ Reflect ▷ Execute

## Collect your stuff

At present you probably have two or three email accounts, post arriving at home and at work, messages on your phone, messages on social media, documents on your desk, scribbles on a notebook (or several), a pad with an important phone number (somewhere), business cards and receipts in your wallet, a draft presentation outline in your laptop case, notes on your phone's notes app, photos of things you think are cool and oh so many brilliant ideas in your head.

So let's start the process by creating a simpler way of gathering new inputs into your life:

— Get all your email into one inbox
— Have one physical in-tray at home and one at work
— Carry a mobile in-tray (I like a zippy mesh folder thing)
— Have one notebook
— Use one app on your phone to collect stuff

Now turn off all notifications — yes, that's right, all of them (OK, we're all allowed one exception). No more badge icons on your phone with 2,000 unread emails, 43 missed calls, 17 Instagram alerts, 62 unread 'read later' articles. No more vibrations. No more beeps. No more unnecessary interruptions. Seize back control. You decide where your attention goes. You are in charge. If people you work with don't like it, tell them that you are doing it so that you can work, create and think better, and if they have a problem with that maybe they need to change! Get tough.

## Arrange it systematically

It is very common that people on a mission to get organised get good at getting tidy but fail to maintain things. The reason is they don't make decisions about it or have a systematic way of going about it. If you follow this simple process with all the inputs in your life, all the time, it becomes a habit. You won't need to remember what to do or even think about it — it becomes your way.

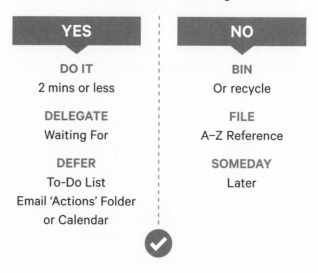

# WORKFLOW
## PROCESS

### INBOX
Do I need to do something?

| YES | NO |
| --- | --- |
| **DO IT**<br>2 mins or less | **BIN**<br>Or recycle |
| **DELEGATE**<br>Waiting For | **FILE**<br>A–Z Reference |
| **DEFER**<br>To-Do List<br>Email 'Actions' Folder<br>or Calendar | **SOMEDAY**<br>Later |

There are two places where I keep track of my 'Actions'.
1. My email 'Actions' folder
2. My to-do lists

The first one is straightforward. The second one can be but often isn't. Again, the typical problem arises when someone thinks more about finding the right tool or app than how they will use it. As these tools can vary in approach and style, very soon you can become overwhelmed with choice, confused and sucked into thinking that the tool, and not you, is the cause or solution to your stress.

So before we look at some tools I have used and recommended, let's look at the keys to creating effective to-do lists.

— **Use verbs!** If you can't start a to-do list with a verb (like write, email, call, find, look for, etc.) you probably haven't worked out the 'action' yet.

— **Add place or context.** By either creating separate lists or using tags for different places you will be able to see what is relevant to where you are. Contexts can be actual physical places (at the office, at home, at the shops) or the resources you need (computer, internet, phone).

— **Create mini-projects.** If something needs more than one action, then highlight this. Decide what the outcome looks like and then list the first three actions at most (no need to overplan). This is a great way to get momentum on the little things of life as well as that big project you still haven't started.

Here's an everyday example:

You need to post a birthday card to a friend so you write on your to-do list, 'Post birthday card to Dylan'. And as the days pass you just don't do it. Why? Because it can't be done. You don't have the card, you don't have a stamp and you don't have his new address. So this is what it should look like, with the relevant place in brackets:

**Mini-Project: Post birthday card to Dylan**

**Actions:**
[  ] Email Dylan to get new address (on the internet)
[  ] Buy birthday card for Dylan (at the shops)
[  ] Buy stamps (at the shops)
[  ] Write card (at the office)
[  ] Post birthday card for Dylan (at the shops)

This might appear overkill and yet there is no other way to get it done. Knowing where your actions are kept means no more piles on your desk hiding things you might need to do, and as a result no more nagging feelings in the back of your mind. And when you look at a clear list of actions when you're in the midst of a crazy day at work, you'll be pleased to find that clarity of action. With no need to think, you just need to do.

More and more people and organisations are moving towards paper-free filing. And yet, have you ever seen a paper-free office? Technology companies are often the worst offenders. In my experience you will need to have a simple way of filing stuff both digitally and physically.

Reference items can be notes, documents, photos, scribbles, magazine articles or just mementos. Clearly labelled and organised filing cabinets are unavoidable. Invest in good ones that will grow with you and avoid temporary solutions like boxes, filing folders and the like that grow into complicated messes, where it's impossible to find anything. This is what I do:

### A simple filing system

**Use one 'A to Z' system for everything**
— family, finances, projects, work, etc.
Avoid vague categories and 'miscellaneous' folders

**Name file folders in an obvious way**
(e.g. 'Insurance–House' or 'House–Insurance')

**Create handy folders on your desk for quick reference**
e.g. 'Action Support' (for documents needed to do things),
'Waiting For' (for things you've delegated or ordered)

If you still end up with piles then make two piles — an 'Action' pile and a 'Reference' pile. Even that simple division will make things a little clearer, both in your outside world and in your mind.

## Reflect on your workload

Every day look at your diary, your to-do lists and your email actions folder *before* you go looking for more work in your inbox. This simple reordering of how you start your day at the computer will put your agenda first. Every week spend at least an hour having a meeting with yourself. Get your physical and email inboxes clear. Run through your commitments — your to-do lists, your projects, your diary for the next two weeks. You can use the review templates to guide you.

## Execute!

Once your mind is clear, and your actions are clear you can do what needs to be done with a lot less friction. You don't need to think twice. You just need to do. Although it can take time to set up, once you have a system in place, your work, your mind and your breath will work a lot more smoothly.

# DAILY REVIEW
## YOUR MORNING ROUTINE

**1**    **CALENDAR** | Schedule
What does your day look like?

**2**    **LISTS** | Today
What's already important?

**3**    **EMAIL** | Action Folder
Are there any existing emails that need action?

Email Inbox
Only look here after the above so you are
aware of all of your present commitments

# WEEKLY REVIEW
## YOUR MOST IMPORTANT MEETING

**1**    **CLEAR THE DECKS**
Process all inboxes to zero

**2**    **SCAN YOUR CALENDAR**
Look back and forwards two weeks
for anything that needs action

**3**    **CHECK ALL YOUR LISTS**
Go through Action and Project lists
Check done items
Add new actions
Chase 'Waiting For' list if required

**4**    **GET PERSPECTIVE**
Review goals and project plans
Reflect on whether your life needs rebalancing
What really matters?

# Tools of a mindful Doer

By standardising your favourite tools and equipment and making sure you always have re-stocks, you will always be ready to do. Here is my basic checklist:

**At my desk**
— A5 notepad
— Great pens
— Index cards for brainstorming
— Filing cabinets
— Tabbed filing folders
— In-tray

**On my computer & smartphone**
— Calendar
— Contacts
— To-do lists
— Documents in the Cloud (e.g. Dropbox)
— Notes
— Writing
— Password manager

**Out and about**
— Pocket notebook
— Zippy A4 folder

Find tools you love to use and stick with them. By being very clear about what you use and why, you reduce mental friction and find more flow and joy in every task. Don't forget to breathe mindfully between tasks! Before switching apps or tasks, take a few breaths from the belly to stay calm and focused.

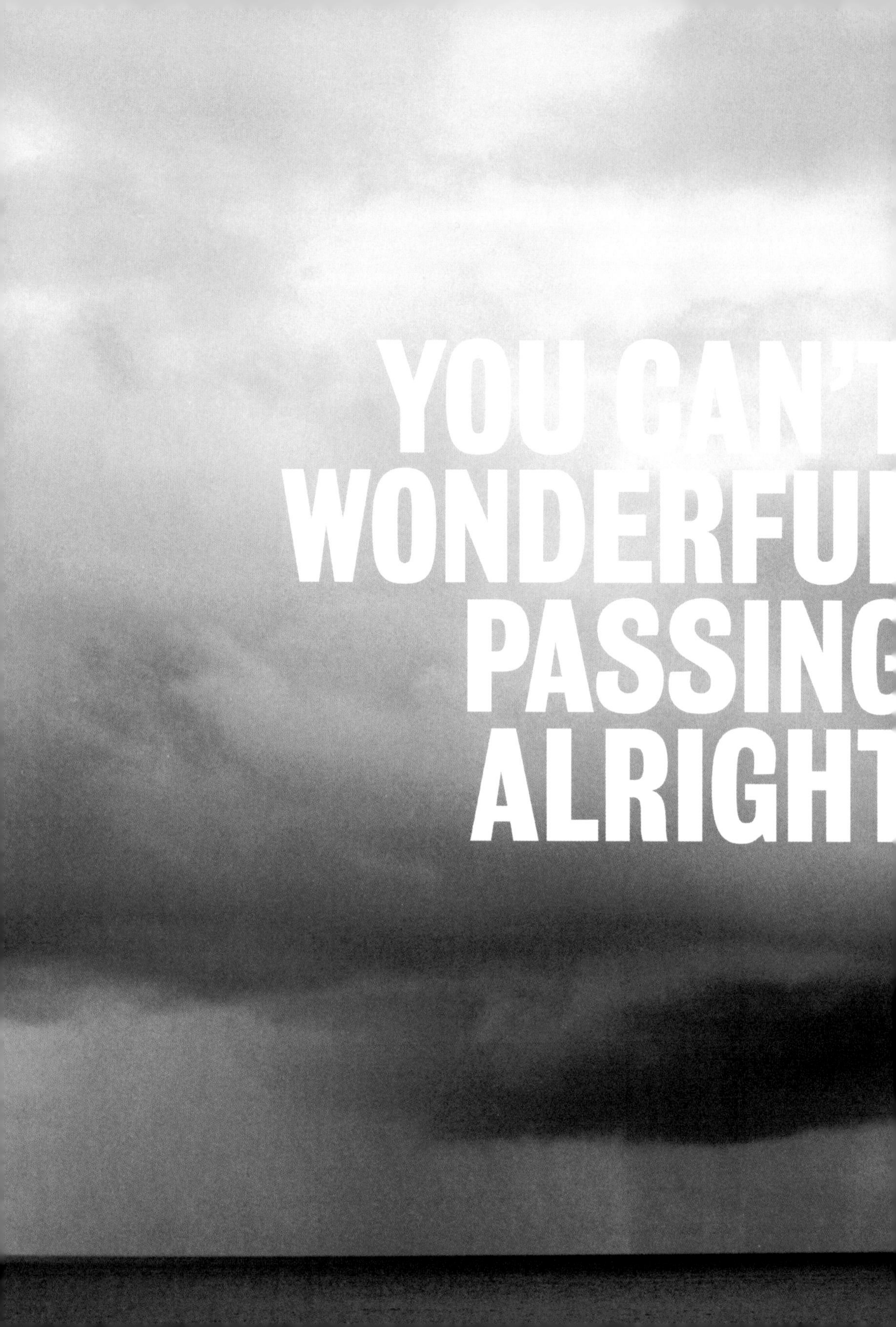

YOU CAN'T
WONDERFUL
PASSING
ALRIGHT

GET TO
WITHOUT
THROUGH

ILL WITHERS

# TEAM

# Even hermits need teams

Unless you're a hermit, you need to be part of a team. Come to think of it, even hermits need teams at some point: maybe to help them build their hermit house, but definitely when they get sick and need to go to hospital. But it's not just a matter of need. Good teams make life happier, more productive, more efficient and more fun. Being a part of a functioning team, wherever you sit in its hierarchy, is truly special. It requires focus, attention to detail and regular adjustment, but the rewards — both individually and collectively — are huge.

This chapter will show you how to get along with everyone you encounter and get the best from them. And, in so doing, build the best team you can.

If you're thinking, 'I pretty much work by myself, I don't need a team,' you're wrong. A team can be two people, or it can be a thousand. You form a team with your accountant and bank manager, with the people you hang out with or play sport with. A team just needs the right human energy at its core. It isn't an inanimate thing; it's a living, breathing organism.

Oh, and one other thing before we start. The biggest mistake I made in business — and it took me years to figure this out — was to try to do everything by myself. Things are different now, so I write from experience.

# The pre-team

When I was at school, and later at university, I loved building teams. I wasn't great at sport, so I'm not talking about anything competitive; mostly I brought people together to make plays, start a band and throw parties. Early on, I saw that when people work well together, they can be truly effective. We were chaotic, confused and hormonal but we did some good things because we had a common goal in sight. Those creative teams were one of the highlights of my education.

Soon after I left university, I got married. Caroline and I were 23 and had met just 16 months earlier. We didn't overthink it. We just did it. Over thirty wonderful years later, this team of two has raised six children, started a festival, opened shops, cafés and holiday cottages, run a pub, co-authored a book, renovated several derelict homes, tried (and often failed) to train endless dogs, and so much more. It hasn't always been easy, far from it. It hasn't always been fun, though there's been a great deal of that, but it has taught us about working together and the power of even the smallest of teams.

A good team isn't a luxury if you want to get stuff done; it's a necessity.

My first career was in the music industry. I was a self-employed music publisher and the manager of a mildly successful pop group. I spent much of this time living in a bubble. I employed a few people but I didn't really engage with them, certainly not emotionally.

At the time, I thought that I had to shield everyone from any worries or concerns to do with the business, to put on a brave face, to figure out problems by myself. I would just ruminate until I came up with a solution.

After a few years it all came crashing down. I was working brutally hard, travelling a lot, stressed and exhausted, and the business had major cashflow issues. And, inevitably, I was often failing as a father and husband. Everything became too much and the business started to collapse.

What I learned was that I should have had a business partner, even a mentor, from the beginning. I had a lovely, very approachable lawyer, but I didn't share any problems with him. With the benefit of hindsight, I know he would have been an excellent mentor or adviser, and I am pretty sure he would have enjoyed acting as one — if only I'd asked him. But, most importantly, I eventually realised that I had a great team working for me but that I didn't work with them.

Over the following years, as I worked on other businesses, I began to change my behaviour. I became more open and honest. I called on others to actually help me with problems and strategy. Piece by piece, we started to build a proper team and, from there, things started to function much better. Today I'd go so far as to say we're thriving.

## First steps

Employing others is a big step. Having staff on payroll is one of your biggest overheads so it's not something to rush into. But there are plenty of ways in which you can build an initial team without having the added stress of paying monthly salaries in the early stages of running a business when cashflow can be unpredictable. Some choose to work with a business partner, sharing investment and equity. Two clever, engaged, hard-working people are often more likely to make a success of a new business than one.

If you don't have someone who would make a suitable business partner, or you'd prefer to develop things yourself for the time being, then do consider having a mentor or some other form of business adviser. Experienced people are often happy to help. These days, I help a lot of people, even if it's just a chat on the phone to talk through an idea. I generally explain that what I have to offer is not a panacea but that I might have something useful to contribute.

The best way to find a mentor is to ask around. See if your parents, friends or friends' parents might know someone who works in a similar industry, or simply has the benefit of accumulated work experience. Then contact them. Don't be shy. Just send them an email introducing yourself and explaining what you're up to and that you would be grateful for any help or insight they might be able to offer. Of course, not everyone will be able or willing to help you, but you'll be surprised by how many people are more than happy to do so. If at first you don't succeed, try someone else.

When you find someone, listen to them and don't demand too much. Prepare for your sessions well and extract the maximum you can from them. I help a few people in this way and I think they find it useful, but — and this is important to remember — I find it enjoyable, rewarding and educational. So, like many of the good things in life, it's win win.

And remember that you probably already have people around you who could be viewed as an early-stage team. People who are working in the wider industry, such as manufacturers, lawyers, accountants, even the nice people in the tax office. Ask them questions. Share your concerns. Don't pretend that everything is hunky-dory when it might not be or things are beyond your comprehension. If you treat them with respect, generosity and honesty, they will repay you with the same.

## One day you'll need to hire someone

If you've worked effectively with your (unofficial) team of mentors and advisers then, one day, when you've started trading and have some money in the bank, and more work than you can cope with, you'll need to employ someone. This is when it gets interesting and you truly need to figure out how to build a proper team and get the best from people.

# EMPLOYEE NUMBER 1

Your culture will attract your people. Nike started life as a running company. It was founded by a runner and a running coach. Its first employee was Jeff Johnson. He was a runner too. That was its culture. They wanted to change running.

Johnson created the first product brochures, print ads and marketing materials, and even shot the photographs for the company's catalogues. He established a mail-order system and opened the first store. He also designed several early Nike shoes, and even conjured up the name Nike in 1971.

Even more than doing all this, he wrote letters to athletes to see how things were going with training. When it came to the Olympics and they had to choose between wearing Adidas or Nike, they chose the one who had taken an interest in their running. Those letters changed Nike's history.

Who is going to be your first hire?

# HIRE SLOWLY

Make the interview last longer. An hour is not enough. You will get to know more about them by setting them a live project. Give them a short deadline. See how they get on. It will tell you so much more than an interview* ever will.

Take them out of the office. Go for a run with them. Have a beer with them. See them as people. If you can't spend time with them, do you really want to hire them?

Remember, a crazy amount of your management time will be spent on a wrong hire. A lot of your stress will come from having to deal with a wrong hire. So can you afford to spend more of your time on making the hiring process longer?
Yup, I think so.

*Introverts don't interview well, but can have the best ideas.

# FIRE QUICKLY

Not every hire works out. And both parties know it quickly. Within three months you know that, well, it isn't going to end well. And yet companies don't act. The person isn't happy. The team isn't happy.* And that can last for years. Decades, even.

Your duty is to the team, the culture and ultimately to the purpose of the company. And, therefore, you have to do the difficult thing quickly.

The person would be happier in another job. The team would be happier with another person. And life is too short for people to be miserable. People make the mistake of being nice, and not dealing with the problem. This means the person is unhappier for longer. It may seem counter-intuitive, but there is a kindness to acting quickly.

*A players prefer to be around A players.

HIRE
HUNGER
OVER
TALENT

In an ideal world you would have both these things in one person. Alas, that isn't always possible. So if you had to choose, I would choose Hunger.

Hunger is always keen to learn. Always trying to get better. Hunger is always putting the extra hours in. Hunger doesn't get lazy.

Over time Hunger works so hard at their thing that their Talent begins to shine above even someone with a natural gift for it. Hunger is normally insecure about their Talent, so continues to work at it. They never lose the Hunger, so just keep putting the practice in. Malcolm Gladwell believes 'Talent is the desire to practise'. I am pretty sure he is right on that.

Indeed Talent comes from the hunger to get better. You can't give people hunger. You can't train it or inspire it. They either have it in their belly or not. It comes with them when they walk in the room. Or not.

Words from *Do Purpose* by David Hieatt

# True leadership

It's commonplace today to hear people talk about a leadership vacuum. And it's true — at the present time we have few real leaders we can look to, and those we do look to for leadership are judged by a low standard.

Look at any sector where we expect to see inspirational leaders — politics, business, entertainment, law enforcement — and instead we see scandal after scandal, each peeling away another layer of our implicit trust in, and respect for, our leaders.

But are there fewer real leaders? Or, as I believe, has the entire concept of leadership been distorted over the last half-century — shifting our perspective and preventing us from seeing acts of true leadership?

When we consider the idea of leadership, we see it as an elite act, set apart from everyday life and undertaken by people who are somehow special. We think leadership is something 'other', something practised by people who are not you, not I.

And, of course, once we 'outsource' the idea of leadership — place it in the hands of these 'others' — two things immediately begin to happen: first, we start to lose trust in the 'others'; and secondly, we get to exempt ourselves from their failures. If leadership is undertaken by people other than ourselves, then their failures are their fault and their problem — not ours.

Whether it's an expenses scandal or obscenely intrusive spying or botched corporate governance or outright fraud, we get to stand aside, wash our hands of the consequences and tut.

It is said that every generation gets the leadership they deserve, and at present we're reaping the consequences of this outsourcing of leadership: our leaders are letting us down, and as a consequence our institutions are failing.

But this doesn't need to be so. Over and over again, I've proved in my own career, working with institutions, organisations and their leaders for three decades, that this slide can be halted, and real, effective leadership restored in almost any environment. It takes only one realisation: leadership isn't an elite act. We can all, any of us, lead at any time. And in fact, more of us should.

# What is leadership?

Let's start with the real secret of leadership: it happens all the time, almost anywhere you look, and it's frankly not that difficult.

Disappointed? Perhaps you were expecting something a little more ... well, challenging? That's not surprising, because for the last, oh, three millennia — in fact, since an unknown Homo erectus first did a Banksy on a cave wall — we've been pretty much preoccupied as a society with the idea of heroic leadership. You know, the Neanderthal who slays the sabre-toothed tiger, Odysseus, Napoleon, the little Dutch boy with his finger in the dyke, Captain Sully, Bobby Moore — all that good stuff.

Which is fine. It makes for good reading and an endless source of uplifting quotes (great for use in motivational posters and filling all that white space left over on your team-building PowerPoint slide).

The problem is that we've become so accustomed to leadership being defined as heroic by journalists (or historians) looking for a good story, we have lost the ability to see true leadership for what it really is: an almost always un-glorious, headline-free, mundane activity that takes place every minute of every day in uncountable different (albeit prosaic) ways.

Like a sports-loving couch potato who has become so addicted to YouTube highlights, instant replays and canned post-game synopses that he can no longer bear the monotony of actually attending (let alone watching) a complete, unedited, in-the-raw football game, we've become accustomed to the media's Hollywood-style version of leadership to such a degree that we have lost our capacity for recognising genuine leadership as it happens around us every day in real life. And when we do that, things start to change.

Don't get me wrong. I have nothing against heroic leadership. In fact, because of my job (I coach senior executives) I'm in a privileged position and get to see more of it than most people. I'm a sucker for heroic acts of leadership. And watching people do incredible things under stress or navigate themselves and others through difficult situations regularly reduces me to a blubbering mess.

But that doesn't mean we should take the 'hero-as-leader' template as our only, or even our main, model of leadership. Real-world leadership is very, very different from all that the media would have us believe. Real-world leadership is most typically understated — often to the point of going unseen by most people. Real-world leadership is most often prosaic, mundane, unspectacular.

Here's my take — one that I've honed from 35 years of working with leaders (heroic and otherwise), and from engaging in occasional acts of leadership myself:

**Leadership is helping any group of two or more people achieve their common goals.**

Not very complicated, I admit, but it's a robust definition that has served me and the people and organisations I work with well over the years. It means anyone can engage in acts of leadership, at any time. In both formal and informal environments. And it means you can lead. Yes, you.

# TRUST BREEDS MAGIC

Tina Roth Eisenberg (better known as @swissmiss) gave a talk at Do USA. She talked a lot about building her amazing companies, and building the team, and the importance of fun. One of the slides that she put up read: **Trust breeds magic.**

Yup, like Tina, I believe in teams. I believe when a team comes together, there is very little that they can't do. But some teams end up fighting each other like crazy, and subsequently, they go the way of the dinosaur. This fascinates me. So why do some teams come together, and others fall apart?

I know, in order to build a business, I have to build a team first. It is one of the key skills that an entrepreneur has to learn. Building a team isn't complex. My learning is that a team is galvanised by two things. Firstly, they like to gather around the founding idea of the company. The more that idea is going to change things, the more people will want to gather around it. Purpose is important.

The second thing teams love to gather around is a leader they trust. Trust is a multiplier of energy for a team. In order for the team to trust the leader, the leader has to show the team that he or she trusts them. Trust is a two-way street.

But most companies are not set up to trust their people. In fact, they are set up to do the opposite. And yet trust is free. It breeds loyalty and passion and helps us all pull together. The magic of trust is that it helps a team to become a team.

# Let's talk about trust

Now you're beginning to build a team. From now on it's *we*, not me. At the heart of that team lies trust. You need to trust them, and they need to trust you. Why? Well, one reason is that to build a great company, you're going to need to start delegating. And in order to do that, you need to trust that the person you are delegating to will get the job done. Also, if you're going to lead people, they have to want you to lead them. So you have to earn their trust. And that's simple enough. You need to be trustworthy.

It's fascinating how many parents think they can tell their children to do one thing, and then do another themselves. If you tell your child not to swear and then swear like a trooper yourself, you're naive if you think that your child won't hear you and copy you. The same thing applies to trust at work. Don't expect others to follow up on commitments if you don't. Life just doesn't work like that.

So do what you say you will do. Turn up on time. Support your team when they're in difficulty. Never say, 'I'm just being honest,' when, in fact, you're just being rude. You have to mean it — you can't say one thing and do another because people aren't stupid. Behave in a trustworthy way and that trust will grow and develop. So, lead by example because you can be trusted.

## Learn to delegate

Once trust has been established, you can start to delegate. If you don't, work on the trust some more. Delegation is often seen as weakness. Calling someone a 'really good delegator' is rarely said without cynicism.

But the best leaders are the best delegators, and to develop your team you're going to have to learn how to achieve this. Really, it's about trust and empowerment. If you trust your team, set them free. Give them tasks you would normally do. Let them learn on the job. Then take a step back.

OK, that's easier said than done. The first thing to remember is that clear instructions are paramount here. Take time to explain what you want and do so precisely and in depth. Don't assume that people will understand what's in your head until you tell them.

## Set your team free

On some levels, I can be a control freak; I suspect many entrepreneurs are built the same way. I have clear, passionately held views on how things need to be done in order for our businesses to move forward. This is good; it's necessary. But in order to be truly efficient, I need to let things go by empowering people around me to get on by themselves. And to achieve this I need to show people how things should be done and then set my team free.

Assuming you've built mutual trust with someone, the thing to do here is to tell them what you want (remember: clear, simple instructions) and let them get on with it. Let them learn on the job, don't micro-manage them and don't interfere. Sometimes things will go horribly wrong, sometimes they will do as good a job as you and sometimes they will do it better.

If it's the former, then gently but firmly correct them. Be clear and precise but don't give up on them. You have to say what is right and explain what's wrong. Do it straight away. Don't baulk at this: praise and criticise with the same directness and kindness that you'd like someone else to show when they speak to you.

So, correct mistakes but be careful not to admonish people who don't approach things in precisely the way you do. One of the magnificent upsides of delegation is that fresh ideas and approaches emerge, and these can be incredibly illuminating. Just because you did something one way doesn't mean that that is the *only* way to do it or, indeed, even the best way. This may bruise the ego a little, but I'm sure you can take it.

With your approval and a little time, the people in your team will become as good as you at a particular task, and then they will become better. And guess what? Once someone else can do those other things, you can then focus on the things you are best at. This is when a team can really start to play to its strengths.

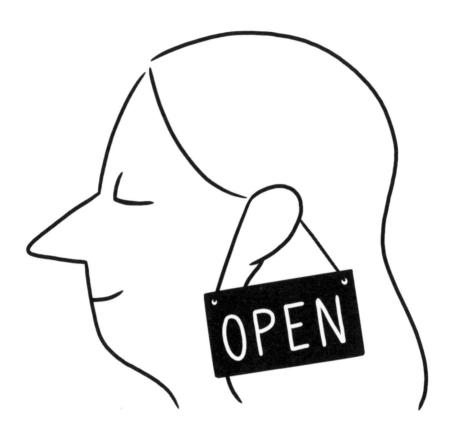

# Gentle leadership

## It takes strength to be gentle and kind

— The Smiths, *I know it's over*

However democratic your company or organisation is, someone needs to be in charge. If hierarchy isn't encouraged, a leader will probably emerge anyway. This section will show how the most effective leadership is about empathy and kindness. Being loud and bossy never got the best from anyone. The best leaders live at the heart of their teams. They get involved, they ask questions, they listen and hang out. They are part of the team. And from there, good things start to happen.

### It's good to talk

There are plenty of employers who think that they don't have time to chat with their team. They're just too busy and important. But they're wrong. A team is an active community, and showing an interest in that community is a critical part of enabling it to function. In short, you need to know quite a lot about the people in your team in order to get the best from everyone.

Fundamentally, people are interesting. So, sometimes, just try and chat. Don't talk about yourself; ask others about themselves. To some this comes naturally, they just want to learn more about those around them. To others it doesn't come so easily but will start to feel more natural over time.

It's actually rewarding to ask people about their lives and to listen to their responses. But remember to *actually* listen — this isn't about paying lip service. So, concentrate! And you know what? This is easy to do because almost everyone is interesting. You just have to have an open mind and be generous with your questions, and give yourself time to listen and respond.

You might think you don't have much in common with someone, but you just need to scratch the surface. If you discover someone in your team has an unusual hobby, train spotting for example, ask them about it: how many books they've filled with numbers, what *compels* them, how many people share their interest. Spark things up. If they sense that your interest is genuine, they'll share their passion and what they tell you will be interesting. Then later, you can continue that conversation and good things will develop between you, and you will like each other, and from that comes your team.

## Have empathy

Everyone is someone's child, girlfriend, husband, best friend, grandchild. Remember this. We all have feelings. Everyone is human and has their own network of loved ones and friends outside the office. These things matter at work as much as they matter anywhere else. So, put yourself in someone else's shoes every now and then.

And remember that you are not any more important than anyone else. You may be the founder or the boss or whatever, but everyone is equal. Everyone is special.

To be a great leader you need to know this to be true.

## Lead by example

Pull, don't push. One of the best ways to help those around you to progress, evolve and blossom in ways that benefit the company is to lead people by example with enthusiasm and energy, rather than pushing them hard.

Positive leadership is rarely about cracking a whip. It's about encouragement and incentive and being a good role model.

Sometimes you'll need to lay down the law, but most of the time you just need to lead people by example, so keep yourself, your mood and your actions in check.

## The power of praise

Isn't it funny how we tend to praise children and not adults? Sometimes it feels as if we're praising children every waking minute, in fact. But rarely do we say to a colleague, 'You did something really remarkable there,' or 'You did a much better job than I would have.'

Praise is oxygen, and not just for children. I read somewhere that people would rather have regular praise from their boss than a pay rise. Who knows, but it's not just a way of saying, 'I see you and I hear you,' but rather, 'I *not only* see and hear you, but think you're doing really well.'

There are theories that praise can trigger the same reward centres in the brain — the ventral striatum and ventral prefrontal cortex — that light up during sex. I have no idea if this is true, but I like it so I'm going to run with it. Without necessarily wishing to turn your office into a seething mass of orgasmic positivity, please do consider handing out praise more often. But only do it when you mean it. Done properly and genuinely, praise will help you to build powerful, trust-based relationships with your colleagues. So don't fake it.

## Be decisive

If you're a team leader (and remember, it doesn't matter how huge or tiny that team is), you need to make decisions, often on the hoof. Don't be afraid of making decisions; someone has to. Teams cannot operate entirely democratically. So, listen to the views of others, weigh things up, then make a decision and let everyone know the new direction of travel. Decision made! Done.

Don't be scared. You are almost certainly not dealing with absolutes here; there is no right or wrong decision. It's what you do once you've made the decision that counts. Sometimes you don't need advice or *more advice*, you just need a decision. So, make one, risk it, move forward.

Great teams need great leaders, and occasionally leaders need to make difficult decisions and tell people what is expected of them. This is leading from the front and it's what your team expect of you. Follow your gut, even if people disagree with you. Sometimes you will need to be forthright, strong and expressive, but you can still remain polite and considerate. My advice is to make a decision and stand by it.

This gets things done. And however gentle and inclusive your normal style is, being more assertive from time to time will serve you well. People want to look up to — and importantly, respect — a team leader. Remember, you can't please all of the people all of the time.

It took me a long time to understand this. I am a people-pleaser; I want to like people and I want them to like me. This isn't a bad thing; it's good to be sensitive. But it can be exhausting, as well as pointless. These days, as long as I'm doing what I believe to be the right thing for the company as a whole, then I have to stand by those decisions. So, don't mumble, don't procrastinate, don't apologise: make a decision and communicate it effectively.

## Be consistent

Consistency of behaviour is critical to great leadership. Leaders need to be adults, by which I mean balanced, calm grown-ups. Understanding the value of consistent behaviour is half the battle. If you can be consistent in the way you communicate, in how you *are*, it makes it a great deal easier for those who work with you to thrive because they will intuitively begin to understand how things should be done. Which brings me on to moods ...

## Control yourself

Given that effective leadership is about leading by example, you need to ensure that you never bring your bad moods into work. Sure, you're going to feel rotten sometimes and have off days. We all do. But as the leader of a team (and that might only be a team of two), you just can't let your moods spill out at work. If you do — and plenty of bosses do — you are simply legitimising moody behaviour in the workplace.

So, learn your moods. Bite your tongue. First, self-awareness. Then self-control.

## The value of gentle, truthful admonishment

Don't avoid conflict. Remember, if something is wrong, you have to say it is. Without learning how to warn or reprimand someone effectively, you will never build a good team. Mistakes are going to be made and if you don't deal with them, they will probably keep happening. Of course, one option is to revert to doing things yourself. But it's far better to speak to the individual or the team as a whole so they improve.

— **Remember that telling someone else they're wrong doesn't always need to mean that you're right.** What you are trying to do is to get your colleague to see the matter in hand in the same way that you do. It's necessary for your business to work efficiently and move forward.

— **Stay calm.** Breathe, take time out, reflect. Remind yourself you're a really good leader. Calmness is power.

— **When you do correct someone, do it clearly, precisely and in detail.** Don't be smug or self-righteous. Explain precisely why you think what they have done is wrong and how they can correct it.

— **Bring some balance to the conversation.** Maybe even temper this admonishment with praise and encouragement, but don't let the balance shift to the positives just because you don't want to hurt someone's feelings. Be honest and be direct. You owe this to the people on your team to help them to grow and evolve. Be a good teacher.

## Changing your mind is not a weakness

In fact, it's a strength. It's about being open-minded. If you're brave enough to change your mind, then you're on the way to becoming a team leader. Good work!

So many politicians have been vilified by journalists for changing their minds that this has now become known as 'doing a U-turn' and is seen as an entirely bad thing. It isn't.

So, allow yourself to change your mind if that's the best course of action — and give your team the freedom to do likewise. This is a natural function of learning and becoming wiser. And it's better to stop a plan now than to linger over something that just doesn't feel right.

## Get over yourself

At work, as at home, never allow yourself to become isolated. Admit your weaknesses and acknowledge the things you forgot, the things you can't handle. Allow your team to see right into you as often as you can. You are human, and so are they, and this will help build unity.

You never really understand
a person until you consider
things from his point of view ...
until you climb into his skin
and walk around in it.

— Atticus Finch, *To Kill a Mockingbird*

# The lost art of listening

## When people talk listen completely

— Ernest Hemingway

Why is it we feel surprised, even grateful, when someone really hears us — when someone leans in and gives us their time and attention? How has this basic act and most primal of senses become such a rare commodity in today's world? Has the one-way street of social media 'broadcasting' really marked the end of conversation and listening?

A US national news channel recently conducted an experiment with a small group of teenagers between fourteen and sixteen years old. The reporter's story was addressing the latest scientific studies that suggest smartphones encourage addictive behaviours, ADHD, depression, FOMO (fear of missing out) and so on. Her experiment was to see what would happen if she took away the teenagers' smartphones and laptops. They were to go cold turkey for one full week.

I expected that the teens would report great resentment, high anxiety and frustration at being cut off. And, of course, some of them did. But they also knew this experiment had an end date. When they were asked how they felt at the end of the week, to the reporter's — and my own — surprise, all of the students responded with what I call 'curious wonder'. They were slightly amazed at how much they enjoyed talking with their families over dinner. They found time for conversation with their friends. They got their homework done, finished their chores — much to their parents' amazement. It is often said that the smartphone has killed small talk as well as the quiet ability to just hang out and learn to handle boredom. When the teens were asked what they took away from this week-long famine of social media connectivity, one fifteen-year-old girl said, 'I really want to stop using my phone, and learn to just *be* with my friends.' Face to face. Not in a group with each person's face pressed into their individual screens. She was genuinely filled with a curious hope.

It's interesting to note that when each of us was in our mother's womb, our eyes were closed but our ears already worked. We heard her heartbeat, the swishing of the amniotic fluid, the jolt of loud noises in the outer world. That was our world. As such, our hearing is connected to our primal emotions and memories. Only when we are born do our eyes open, gather focus and take in all the light and tonal differences of this new world. Since our eyes are on the front of our face, our main reference point from then on is visual — our perspective is usually based on whatever our eyes can see. Listening retreats to the periphery, a dancing shadow, insofar as our perception is concerned. But it remains the ambient light of our emotions, hard-wired to our first feelings. From the time our ears are formed, they remain on, 24/7. Our hearing is our last sense to go when we die. This is why the Greeks said that our ears are the 'guardian of our sleep'. A mother will hear her baby cry in the dead of night.

Medical science has discovered that the minute hair fibres lining the cochlea in our ear canal contract and expand, similarly to the irises of our eyes. They do so in response to sound waves coming in. Our ears are alerting and protecting us as best they can, but ever since the Industrial Age, our ears have been under assault. Now, we close our ears to all the overlapping, nonstop sonic intrusions. We are selective — choosing to block out the natural world with our headphones, empowered to choose what we want to hear. But in doing so, we are no longer able to sense what is calling us. We have lost the ability to listen. We have forgotten —

if we ever knew — the power of silence. We cannot remember how the birds and animals speak — and why we even need to know what they are saying.

Listening is a gift — one we give to ourselves and also to others. When you listen, you always get far more back than you had going into the conversation. Simply put, you know more. I know full well what it's like to live in the oxygen-deprived presence of someone who loves the sound of their own voice, and I bet many of us are familiar with the feeling of being obligated to listen to someone due to their power over us — be that a family member, a boss, or any superior. You become numb by repeated exposure.

But listening does not have to be boring. Think of it as choosing to be in tune with others. It has been said that the problem with our current social media landscape is that we are each living in our own silos, each of us in our own self-selected 'filter bubbles'. We only want to listen to those who are like us.

But if we choose to not listen to what makes us uncomfortable, how will we ever grow? How can a democracy exist without debate, negotiation and compromise? Our current democratic process might appear to be broken beyond repair, but there is still much of value in its ideals.

Listening takes time. You must pause, take a moment and offer yourself to another person, with your full attention. Honestly, sometimes this can feel like a drag. Maybe their issue will inconvenience you. Maybe they're confused or in emotional pain. But there will be times when listening will be the most important thing you will ever do.

# The hidden world reveals itself when we listen

### Exercise: A 5-minute listening practice

Someone once said that we should never underestimate the 5-minute conversation with a 16-year-old. Can you find 5 minutes to give to someone — perhaps someone you know you should listen to more, or someone who simply needs your time and focus, even just for a few minutes? Simply listen to the other person without judging, or reacting with your eyes or sighs or any audible reactions.

See what happens ...

# Muhammad Ali's best poem

Muhammad Ali was once asked what his shortest poem was. He replied in two words: 'Me, We'.

In these two short words Ali gave insight into our true human nature. We need to be truly ourselves as individuals, but we can only be so when connected to a greater 'We'. The Me needs the We to create more than is possible as an individual; and the We needs Me — every Me — to come with their full capacity to create meaning collectively.

'We' is how we create narrative, culture, context and meaning — it's the glue that binds us. Strip a community or a business of the means to create We, and we all suffer as a result.

For a while we forgot the We, and got hung up on the Me, Me, Me a bit too much.

But if you want vibrancy in your business, vibrancy in your community, I would read Ali's shortest, and perhaps his best, poem again and again and again until it becomes a mantra.

# People embrace
# what they create

People embrace what they create with love, with energy, with passion. They are prepared to go the extra mile. Their work becomes a labour of love — for we as people do not labour for monetary reward, we labour for meaning.

So whether leading a team, or running a workshop, ensure people are the true co-creators of their future, that they are heard and listened to. That is a very different energy and motivation from barking orders and telling people what to do. And you'll probably find people are less stressed, take fewer days off work and the workplace becomes a cultural hub of vibrancy and energy.

When people are co-creators they become part of a narrative that runs through a business. They become part of its story.

As French writer Saint-Exupéry put it, 'If you want to build a ship, don't give out orders and tell people exactly what to do. Teach them to yearn for the vast and endless sea.' The rest, I believe, will take care of itself.

I am all for helping others yearn for the vast and endless sea.

# CREATIVITY

# A creative response

Creativity sets humans apart. Everything we make or do depends on our creative history. From stone axes to supercolliders, the ability to create, for ourselves, is one of our defining characteristics.

From axes we moved on to fire, arrows, pots, agriculture, cooking, recipes, cuisine, nouvelle cuisine and so on, all the way up to the celebrity chef. Along the way we created language, art, science, philosophy and rubbish bags with little drawstrings that make them easier to close (one of my personal favourites). By being creative we have shaped and fashioned the world around us to an enormous extent. Creativity is an important part of what makes us human.

If creativity is our past, it is also our present. In our everyday lives we constantly face threats and opportunities we cannot anticipate, that require (or invite) a creative response from all of us. The pandemic that was unleashed in 2020 brought that home in a dramatic way, on a large scale. It is more obvious than ever how important it is to be able to adapt. There *will* be another pandemic and it won't look like the last one. We won't be able to cut and paste from the past, so the kind of future we have will depend upon our capacity to be creative.

We also have to find ways to clear up the mess produced by the industrial 'solutions' of yesterday without producing yet more toxic waste, squandering energy or destroying the ecosystems on which we depend to grow food, cycle water or produce oxygen. Just doing less of what we currently do won't be enough. To navigate climate change we need to be creative on a scale that has never been seen before. The problem is vast, complex and new, so we don't have the solutions — we have to create them.

In a 2006 TED talk that has received 72 million views, Sir Ken Robinson argued that creativity is the new literacy. It is *that* important. In a global economy, driven by rapid technological change, creativity at every level is fundamental. Organisations of all kinds, including governments, businesses and NGOs, constantly need to serve people in new ways as their needs and interests shift. They might have to create new services or products, find new ways to deliver old ones or reinvent themselves completely.

The same is true for individuals, who need to be creative not just to keep themselves employable but in order to shape their lives, which will not proceed along the predictable, professional paths that they used to. As Robinson points out, most of the children in school today will do jobs that haven't been invented yet. This hasn't happened before.

Furthermore, all the most interesting and important human dilemmas, like how to reconcile liberty and security, are problems that we never 'solve'. Instead of settling on single answers, we have to come up with a stream of creative responses, as we adapt anew to changing circumstances. The world does not stay still; we are forever responding to all the complexity of life.

Creativity isn't just about solving problems either. It is important to the quality of our everyday experience. Being involved in a creative process brings joy and delight to those participating as well as those who benefit from it. This is not the sole preserve of artists or Nobel Prize winners. Psychologist Mihaly Csikszentmihalyi, who has dedicated his career to the study of happiness and creativity, argues that 'to have a good life it is not enough to remove what is wrong with it'. Happiness, it seems, is about more than solving problems. In order to be happy, we need to find ways to express and develop our creativity. Creativity, it turns out, matters an awful lot.

# Co-creation

Given this importance, it is worrisome that the popular image of creativity is about as misleading as it is widespread. Ask most people to conjure up an idea of someone creative and it's likely they will come up with a version of the 'eccentric inventor' or 'artist in his garret'. The image is of a lone individual, of rare talent, engaged in a tortuous process of creation, with inspiration occurring in blinding flashes.

There are two striking features of this image. First, it is not a very accurate depiction of how creativity occurs, either in the arts or in science (or, for that matter, in business). Secondly, it depicts creative people as 'other'. They are disconnected and separate.

If this is the image you have, it is unlikely you will think of yourself as creative. Which is inhibiting. It stops you being, or becoming, as creative as you might. To paraphrase Henry Ford — if you believe you aren't creative, you'll be right. We need to debunk this image.

Let's start with the pain. It may indeed be difficult to make a living as an *artist*, but that doesn't mean the *creative* process itself is a necessarily painful one. Struggle may be involved, but in many ways, play is more important to creativity than pain. Improvisers have an enormous amount of fun while they create. It's a large part of why they do it.

The idea that you are born creative (or not) is another unhelpful one. I often hear professional creative people promote it. This is hardly surprising, since it makes them 'special'. However, for those who aren't professional creatives, it sets up a self-fulfilling prophecy. If creativity is an innate talent, you would be a fool to try and develop it, so, lo and behold, you don't. It is more helpful to think like the ancient Greeks. They suggested that people were 'visited' by the muse. For centuries, inspiration was a touch of the divine. It came and went. It was neither a talent, nor a possession — it wasn't yours alone.

In fact, this is much more accurate than creativity being regarded as a special, individual talent. Creative people rarely work in isolation. There is always a milieu — a movement or a community of some kind, where ideas are sparked off, exchanged, cross-fertilised and tested. This may be informal, like the coffee houses of 17th-century London, or formal, like the modern scientific peer-review process, but one way or another, there is interaction between people and their ideas.

This is very obvious with improvisers, whose creative process is visibly collective, but even when someone appears to be isolated, they still interact with other people's ideas, through reading or correspondence. It is neat and tidy to attribute acts of creation to individuals (and it may suit the individuals concerned), but there is almost always a collaborative element. The individual is always in a context — and ideas emerge from the relationships between the people who operate in that context.

# Start making again

Hands, fingers, fingerprints. We all have our own unique conduit through which we connect to the physical world.

I feel the deepest connection to the earth when I'm walking beneath a rich, luscious woodland canopy and I run my hand over the topography of tree bark. Or when I'm surfing in the ocean engulfed by a beautifully dynamic energy, stroking my hands through the cold, salty, swirling water. Two awe-inspiring spaces that exist on our incredible planet, connected to each other and to me, through my senses, through my hands.

As a maker, taking a raw piece of timber through a creative process of physical change allows me to connect back to the earth, back to the ocean and back to myself. Through the act of making, we reawaken our hands and minds to reconnect with the beauty of the natural world around us. Making allows us to slow down, offers an opportunity to grow in confidence and can lead to a deeper sense of purpose.

It is an instinctive and intrinsic part of all of us that many have lost touch with. We just need the support, encouragement and confidence to get started again.

# Every child is an artist. The problem is how to remain an artist once they grow up.

— Pablo Picasso

When was the last time you created something you were willing to put your name to? How far back do you have to go? Yesterday, last week, last year… maybe even back to school? If you cast your mind back to your childhood, do you have memories of making and creating? Clicking Lego pieces together, digging your fingers into Play-Doh, or running them through paints and across pieces of paper?

When we are children, play and creation seem to go hand-in-hand. Through play, we interact with the world around us and become aware of our own sense of uniqueness. The marks we make on a piece of paper with our fingers dipped in paint, the shapes we squeeze and mould out of dough and the structures we build by clicking blocks together have come to exist through us and our hands. In their own small way, they stand as a physical representation of how we have made our mark on the world around us. And as children, we have no problem presenting them to the world: 'Mum! Dad! Look what I made!'

Those early memories will almost always be connected to a person or people with whom the experience is shared — a parent, sibling, teacher or best friend. With these people, we are exploring our impact on the world, collaborating and interacting to create shared visions. They are also the people whose judgement ultimately has the strongest impact on what we decide to do next.

The reason we all struggle to remain artists as we grow up is that we learn to fear judgement. We get caught up in trying to create something that's perfect, so it isn't judged negatively. At school, especially, when we start to compare our creations with those of our friends, we begin to believe the story that maybe we aren't quite good enough. That perhaps our talents lie elsewhere. So gradually we stop creating. We stop making.

In order to create and make again, we need to understand how to release ourselves from the judgement of others and, more importantly, of ourselves. We need to see that the pursuit of perfection is not a healthy one. We must recognise the story that we are telling ourselves — the one we are now living — and work out how that needs to change in order for us to believe that we can do things. We can be creative. We *can* make things.

The idea of craftsmanship is to continually work on a process, seeking perfection through a feedback loop that requires judgement from yourself, while acknowledging that true perfection is unattainable. So craftsmanship is a celebration of judgement and an intrinsic understanding that things will be 'wrong', yet we do them anyway.

Anthropologist Alice Roberts once said that we humans are thinkers and makers and those two things combine uniquely in our species.

For me, the two things are inextricably linked. The act of making, actively using our hands, gives us the opportunity to think. It creates a point of focus for the conscious mind and the physical body that allows space for the subconscious mind to wander, much like in meditation. As a result, it is recognised as a process that can be used for therapeutic purposes. In fact, the practice of occupational therapy was born from the Arts and Crafts Movement of the late 19th century, which actively promoted a return to handcrafting as a response to industrialised production.

Yet here we are, almost 150 years later, and as a society we are even more disconnected from our hands, from materials and from the earth. However, the connection isn't completely lost. Creativity is very much all around us. More than likely you are practising it already.

Do you remember the last time you tried a new recipe, when you cracked open a favourite cookbook and thumbed your way through its pages until something jumped out that you wanted to try and recreate? You followed the instructions as best you could, step by step, likely adding your own twist by replacing an ingredient with something you actually had in the cupboard. Smelling and tasting it as you went to try to get a sense of where the dish was headed. You tried to wrap your tongue and taste buds around the flavours that were being filtered through your senses until, excitedly and nervously, you dished it out onto a plate.

As you ate, weren't you often wondering if it might have been a little more tender if you'd taken it off the heat sooner, or maybe the sauce would have been richer in flavour and texture if you'd left it to simmer for a few more minutes? Whatever happened, you'll either have created a delicious meal and discovered new ingredients and a process that you will replicate another time, or accepted it's not the best thing you've ever eaten and you'll look to find ways to improve it next time. Whatever the outcome, you gave it a go and most likely learned something to enrich your understanding.

> **Humans do two things that make us unique from all other animals: we use tools and we tell stories. When you make something, you're doing both at once.**
> — Adam Savage

Working with raw materials to produce something that didn't exist before, in this case ingredients to create a meal, is a form of making that most of us engage in on a daily basis. Taking those materials through a process that delivers a desirable outcome may seem basic, but it can be incredibly rewarding. If the headspace and sense of satisfaction that cooking gives us can be celebrated and enjoyed, making something — *anything* — will benefit our mood. In fact, engaging in this kind of meaningful, practical activity is not only of benefit, but essential to good mental health, and making doesn't need to stop at the morning cup of coffee or the evening meal.

Now more than ever, as a society — as human beings — we need to recognise the physical and mental benefits of making, support and encourage each other to give it greater prominence in our lives and create time for regular practice.

When we were children, making came naturally. All we need is the space, encouragement and confidence to get started again.

# Pace

The concept of pace was first introduced to me when I was learning how to draw. At the time, I was frustrated that my work wasn't progressing as quickly as other kids in my classroom, so my parents suggested that I slow down and fully understand what I was looking to accomplish before I sped off to do it. (As it turned out, not everything in life was a race — even for us competitive types.) Even as a young kid, this philosophy helped me. It taught me to focus my attention, give myself time to craft my ideas and not rush through something for the sake of getting to a finished product. Unsurprisingly, this lesson came up several times in my upbringing, and it is something that I continue to practise in my creative work and throughout my life today.

Pace is the tempo at which we make things. And from my experience, a slower pace simply yields greater things. When you take your time on a task, project or idea, you become more aware — of yourself, your surroundings and how you fit into everything that's going on around you. It allows you to assess all aspects of your internal and external environments, be proactive in your creative approach and, ultimately, make better decisions. And when it comes to photography, making better decisions is what leads to capturing the right moments — the ones that are notoriously easy to miss if you're moving too quickly.

Though we don't always have the luxury of controlling how much time we have on a given project, we are always able to control the speed at which we think and move. If we quicken our pace, it often results in stress and tunnel vision, which can negatively affect the mood of a shoot as well as its outcome. But if we keep our minds and our movements steady, we create an atmosphere that is comfortable for both ourselves and our subjects — which, in turn, allows us to make the most of the time we do have. In this sense, it's actually a bit of a time-hack.

Technology has enabled us to move and shoot quickly, to make digital piles of pictures as we search for the perfect frame, the perfect subject, the perfect moment. But no matter what we choose to shoot with, the point of photography remains the same: to connect with and capture life as it is, in real-time, with all of its incredible imperfection. This isn't to say that shooting with the latest technology is a bad thing — it just comes with its own set of challenges in terms of pace.

I've personally found that shooting film naturally encourages you to slow down. Because film has such a tactile element to it — from loading to winding to processing — it inspires a pause at every step. It doesn't make it easy (or cheap) to snap photos furiously, so the alternative is careful consideration. It prompts you to set a focus, amble and take the entirety of a scene into account — all the while, quietly teaching you to learn when the right moments are to press the shutter. It's really quite rhythmic. That said, regardless of whether you choose to shoot digital or analogue, if you stay rooted in a slow, easy pace, you'll instinctively learn to make the most of every moment.

Several years ago, I shot a project for Levi's with artist Evan Hecox (see page 164), whom I'd known for some time and had photographed before. While it was great to have an established sense of comfort and familiarity between us, I had never photographed Evan for a specific need or at someone else's creative request. Because we were shooting a brand campaign,

I had to completely rethink how I wanted to photograph him, and contemplate how that approach could also showcase Levi's and its product. This was new territory for both Evan and me — in the past, my eyes had always been focused on his hands, his face, the visual work he was creating. This time, I had to focus on his form and the clothes he was wearing. I was fortunate enough to have a couple of days with Evan in his studio, so I was able to pace myself and really watch how he went about his work. This allowed me to begin to spot the moments when I could capture him authentically and still feature the product (in this case, his jeans). After a while, I began to notice that every time a record would end, Evan would walk over to his record player, squat down and put on a new one. It was a commonplace act that we may not have thought anything of, but those modest vignettes ended up being the perfect times to capture him in an organic way, when he was comfortable and his real habits naturally featured the jeans.

Slowing down in this way gives us added time to understand the whole picture. When we pace ourselves before we fully commit to a creative idea, it helps us not to overthink, over-do or under-deliver — in the end, it's what leads to fewer mistakes and less time wasted. In this particular case, keeping an even pace enabled me to work with Evan in a new way that showcased both his work and the jeans in scenarios that made sense, without pushing him to do things he wouldn't normally do.

# An active pause

A pause is not nothing. Something happens in a pause, or as a result of one. Thus, pausing is different from stopping. Improviser Gary Hirsch describes it as 'a quality of stopping that makes another kind of thinking possible'. Film-maker David Keating talks about a pause as a 'sweet emptiness'. At a material level, it simply isn't possible for there to be nothing happening, even in a pause. As choreographer and yoga teacher Kay Scorah points out, to stand very still you need to be constantly moving, making tiny adjustments to posture and position. Such 'stillness' is compelling to watch, as the street entertainers posing as statues in cities all over the world demonstrate. Look closely and there is always something going on. When you pause you are still thinking, breathing, metabolising.

Even in meditation, there is not nothing. For meditation teacher Rachel Lebus, stilling or emptying the mind is not the aim; meditation is not an instrument of control. Images and thoughts inevitably arise, and the meditation consists of letting them go, not of not having them. In meditation there may be a different quality of mind, but the mind is not entirely empty or still. There is not nothing.

Composer John Cage's most famous and controversial work is entitled *4'33"*. In this piece the performer, or performers, are instructed not to play (for four minutes and thirty-three seconds). Cage's point is that there is never complete silence, that 'everything we do is music'. Similarly, pause is not an absence, but an opportunity to be present to what we would otherwise miss or ignore, in the same way that during *4′33″* the 'music' of the background noise that surrounds us all the time appears. A pause, rather than being nothing, is a switch of attention and activity, from one thing to another. It is 'a "not doing" in order for something else to be done', says actor and singer Phyllida Hancock. We may absent ourselves from the usual stuff, but as we do so, we pay attention to something else.

There is a conundrum here, which points to the difference between people and machines. Author and columnist Dov Seidman sums it up beautifully: 'When you press the pause button on a machine it stops. But when you press the pause button on human beings, they start.'

Since you never know what it is that might start, pause makes an important contribution to creativity. There are patterns to creative processes. One of the patterns that people who study creativity observe is that there is always a discontinuity, or gap, or delay. In short — a pause.

For example, in *Where Good Ideas Come From*, Steven Johnson talks of the 'slow hunch'. He argues that new ideas are 'fragile creatures, easily lost to the more pressing needs of day-to-day issues'. Slow hunches don't develop if you work relentlessly on a problem. They are 'less a matter of perspiration than cultivation' and, like a crop, require fallow periods. It is a living process, not a mechanical one.

Creative director Jack Foster, in *How to Get Ideas*, is explicit about this. He has 'Forget about it' as one of the stages of his idea-generation process. He cites fellow ad man James Webb Young's 1934 classic *A Technique for Producing Ideas*, as well as the German philosopher Helmholtz and a number of academic researchers.

All of them include a stage of disconnection from the task at hand. They may call it 'mental digestion' or 'incubation' but the creative process, however you look at it, has some kind of pause built into it. You don't get to novelty directly.

Often, it is in the pause that the 'eureka moments' occur. These days more people seem to have their ideas in the shower than the bath, but that probably just reflects the change in bathing habits. The drama of the 'eureka' moments makes for a good story, so sudden inspiration often gets most of the attention, but without the pregnant pause that gave birth to them, there would be no such moments at all.

My life has been shaped by serendipitous moments that happened in an 'in-between' time. I met my wife on a day when a tube strike had paralysed the city of Madrid. Hanging out in Portland, Oregon, for no particular reason, led to me starting a business. Such 'radical serendipities' don't happen when you are head down, rushing to a predetermined destination, or buried up to your eyebrows in everyday detail. The opportunities might still be there, but chances are you won't see or notice them, and even if you do, you are likely to dismiss them as impossible while you speed along the path you have planned. As my friend Jorge Alvarez puts it: 'motorways always lead to known destinations'.

Pause undoes the
technology-driven
flattening of time
and gives it back
some depth

# Tell us your story

Stories are the fire we carry to each other. In Cormac McCarthy's novel *No Country for Old Men*, Sheriff Bell recalls that his cowboy father would carry the embers from the fire of one camp to the next in an animal horn. It was a tradition passed to the cowboys by the Native Americans. In the novel, this important act had another meaning: to have hope and continue the quest, but also to maintain humanity. The fire carrier would hold a special position in the tribe and for their society.

Stories possess a spark, a power: to comfort, connect, destroy, transform — and even to heal. Everyone has a story to tell. And everyone can appreciate a great story well told. But we are not all gifted storytellers. However, in all my years of teaching 'The Art of Storytelling' around the world, I have never known anyone to fail at learning how to tell their story, beautifully. Storytelling, as you will see, is elemental within each of us.

The very act of telling your story possesses power. It is through the act of telling and hearing stories that we become inspired. We can envisage a better life for ourselves. The end result is, in fact, that we become courageous. Then, a curious thing happens. Our actions — our individual acts of courage — are what lead to 'healing in the land', that is, the transformation of our world.

Equally powerful is the inverse. The power of storytelling can be lethal. The fact is, history has shown us that stories not told can become like an evil genie left in a bottle. When they are finally uncorked, their power to destroy is unleashed.

———————

What all great stories have in common is a journey whose conclusion appears uncertain. They are full of hope. And they are about courage. The tragic ones are about someone who did not have the courage to do something they had to do, or who took the coward's way out.

This is how we connect to our humanity, and become better people. How well you tell your story can make the difference to anything you do — whether that's convincing someone to love you, buy something you've made, or give something of themselves; or how well you make your way in the world; or, simply, in sharing who you are.

I enjoy sharing the stories of my heroes — the world famous and those known only to a relative few. But the greater stories, to me, may well be the personal ones told by my students, each one of them unique, emotional and memorable. This, in part, is because I had the great pleasure of observing them as they all learned to tell these stories. Storytelling is native to all of us. We just need to do it. Dare to be personal. Dare to be vulnerable. And dare to listen to others sharing their stories.

And, why should you do this? Risk your vulnerability? Because in this age of content creation, someone is telling a story all the time. In fact, we are immersed in them, and even make life choices because of them. Thus, it is necessary for us to harness our own stories, and tell them well. If not, then someone else will come in and wallpaper our culture with their stories. And then, how do we pass on to the next generation what has been lost, if not forgotten?

Remember Churchill: never, ever forget. In the end, all you have is your story.

Tell us your story.

Do.

# The 10 Principles of Storytelling

1 **Tell your story as if you're telling it to a friend**
This applies no matter where you are or who your audience is.

2 **Set the GPS**
Give the place, time, setting and any relevant context.
Keep it factual, short and sweet.

3 **Action!**
Use active verbs or, as I like to say, 'Think Hemingway': spice up your verb choices but keep them succinct. Invest in a thesaurus (or a free app). Avoid multisyllabic, erudite, four-dollar words, over-intellectualising, philosophising, qualifying. See how many I just used? It's boring to read them all, isn't it?

4 **Juxtapose**
Take two ideas, images or thoughts and place them together. Let them collide. Remember German philosopher Hegel here: in posing two opposing ideas, a whole new idea is created (thesis + antithesis = synthesis). This tool wakes up your audience, and is the root of all successful stories.

5 **Gleaming detail**
Choose one ordinary moment or object that becomes a 'gleaming detail'. Something that best captures and embodies the essence of the story. Make the ordinary extraordinary.

6 **Hand over the spark**
Reflect on the experience or idea that originally captivated you and simply hand it to your audience as if it were aflame. Carry the fire.

7 **Be vulnerable**

Dare to share the emotion of your story. Be unafraid to ask your audience what you questioned along the way so they share your doubt, confusion, anger, sorrow, insight, glee, delight, joy, epiphany.

8 **Tune in to your sense memory**

Choose the strongest of the five senses in your story and use it to make a deeper connection with your audience. There is always one primary sense that dominates every memory.

9 **Bring yourself**

A story is as much about you as anything else.

10 **Let go**

Hand over your story, letting it build to its natural, emotional punchline, then end it and get out fast. Leave the audience wanting more. Less is more.

# The gleaming detail

## It's the little things

— Vincent Vega, *Pulp Fiction*

To make a story unforgettable, you need to find that one image that connects with the audience, that 'Aha!' moment. This creates the epiphany we seek in a great story — that surprise revelation or sigh of recognition. This singular image, well positioned, can elevate a story from good ... to great. We call this the 'gleaming detail' — a term originally derived from that great nation of storytellers, the Irish — the element that makes a story stand out.

The gleaming detail is the one thing that captures both the emotion and idea of the story at once, in one fell swoop. A singular, elegant moment of clarity. It is a literal representation of the truth that is inherent within every story. So as you develop your story, ask yourself: what is the truth within the story that I want to tell?

Working this way, your story's own unique gleaming detail may well present itself. First of all, listen to what the story is telling you. Usually, the essence of the story will reveal itself in an ordinary detail — the simple act of sharing tea, for example. Go with this. Don't overthink it. Quite often the more ordinary the detail, the greater or more 'extraordinary' the truth that is revealed.

To give you an example, a student of mine from Denmark told my class the story of her grandmother Helga, her father's mother.

In the late 1940s, Helga went to court to appeal for a divorce on the grounds of 'intolerable cruelty'. This was at a time when no woman dared to divorce her husband and risk her financial future.

Helga and her husband were well-respected members of a Catholic community. They had two young sons, aged three and five, and lived in a fine home. They were prosperous. However, events drove Helga to appeal for divorce. She was forced to plead her own case to the judge because no lawyer wanted to be associated with a woman. In the end, the judge did grant Helga a divorce, but not before he took the opportunity to publicly berate her, asserting that her commitment to this course of action revealed her poor character. She must be a weak wife, an extremely disappointing example of a mother. He pitied her sons and, purely to grant them stability, he awarded Helga the home. When Helga finally left the court and returned to the house, she opened the door and found it entirely empty. While she had been at court all day (being humiliated by the judge), every single item had been removed: all the furniture, the wardrobes full of clothes, the beds, the children's toys, the lights. Even the light sockets had been ripped out of the walls.

In this brief story, universal in its heartache, we are given one 'gleaming detail' that shows us what might have motivated this woman to endure the public humiliation of a divorce. With the image of the ripped-out light sockets, we can fully understand her desperate need to separate herself from a petty, vindictive man who would deny his own children not only their toys, but electricity — light and warmth. This ordinary detail explains the story's hidden truth: Helga's emotional despair. The image of ripped-out light sockets shows us how extraordinarily heartless her home had become. We are moved to compassion for her, and now feel admiration for her courage.

Notice that I set up the story with a brief headline: a woman's appeal for divorce in the 1940s when it was unusual, and a huge financial risk. You, the audience, are given the simplest of facts. There is no judgement about her husband. In the first instance, no reasons are given for her course of action. All we are told is that Helga put herself out on a limb and, in doing so, endured a public harangue from the judge. As the story continues we follow

Helga home and discover that everything that could make a home habitable is gone — their clothes, furniture, even the children's toys. When it comes to the light fixtures we are left asking, who would take the time to rip light sockets out?

Today, part of the problem is that we have had our emotional radar dulled. We are less sensitive to the smaller details and feel we have to spoon-feed our audience. To fill in the blanks for them. Many storytellers think it impressive to qualify tales with flowery adverbs or politically correct statements. Consider this retelling of the same story: 'Now this will be a terribly hard experience for you to imagine, but this is the story of a woman whose husband was bitterly vindictive and made her home life so difficult she was driven to desperate measures.' And then we might have ended the story with, 'That goes to show just how mean a husband and father he was that the first priority for his wife, now destitute, would be to source and pay for an expensive electrician,' and so on.

You don't need to do this. Don't qualify, justify or explain. Simply tell the story. And leave the emotional impact to resound as it no doubt will. The key here is to use the gleaming detail as a device, and to use it sparingly. It should never dominate or become obvious as a storytelling device. Be economical with it. Position it only once or twice so that it will stand out.

# The curious mind is the wellspring of creativity

John Steinbeck wrote in *East of Eden*, 'The free, exploring mind of the individual human is the most valuable thing in the world.'

Curiosity doesn't like rules, or, at least, it assumes that all rules are provisional. It rejects the approved pathways, preferring diversions, unplanned excursions, impulsive left turns. Curiosity is voracious — the more you know, the more you want to know; the more connections you make between the different bits of knowledge; the more ideas you have. Which is why curiosity is really the wellspring of creativity.

If you really push your curiosity you will find yourself, as Galileo, Charles Darwin and Steve Jobs did, rubbing up against fixed orthodoxies that asserted their regal, legal, political or religious authority trying to stop these disruptors' momentum and more importantly devalue their newly acquired authority. Not that these three adventurers did too badly out of it ... eventually. They brought beauty and a more beautiful way of being, and knowing, to the world.

To be and to remain deeply intensely curious about our world is vital to original thinking, whereas the incurious face a rather dim future. To have a hungry heart and mind determines what it is we create.

# Try making an appointment with serendipity

Have you ever received an invitation from serendipity in the post or via email? It says, 'Dear xxx, I hope you are well? I would love to invite you to a moment of profound serendipity, say this Friday coming. We can have a lovely lunch and chat about those amazing insights I am going to give you. Don't be late. Love, Serendipity.'

No, serendipity never makes an appointment — she just arrives, in whatever fashion is her wont. She might jab the hand of God through the clouds, or she might decide the smallest, quietest whisper is all that is needed to nudge you along and reveal the insights you already hold.

So always leave the door open for a little serendipity, because you never know when it will turn up, unannounced. With your depth of field and curious soul, allowing something to evolve or seeing meaning in playful accidents can make the difference between creating the same old thing, or something that is unique, valuable, lasting, beautiful.

Sometimes it's better not to try at all; just let things come. Only be ready to surrender your heart to serendipity's will.

# Making ourselves

**When you get rid of your fear of failure, your tensions about succeeding ... you can be yourself. Relaxed. You'll no longer be driving with your brakes on.**

— Anthony de Mello

I feel so lucky to have found something that I was passionate about at such a young age. I was able, with love and support from those around me, to follow that passion and carry it with me. The path that has led me here has been guided by my love for people and the environment, so I would implore you to do the same. Follow your heart and stick to what you enjoy, because you'll end up living a life you love.

For various reasons, but mostly because I was challenged recently by a close friend, I started to question where this passion and direction came from. The friend encouraged me to dig deep and I found that underneath everything that we experience, if we strip it all away, we are left with love. At our core, we all have love and compassion for the planet, love for each other and love for ourselves. Making something can be a great reminder of this.

Whilst I was writing my book, it became impossible to ignore the parallels between the process of making a physical object with our own two hands, and that of making ourselves.

You could say that we all enter this world as a blank canvas, an empty vessel. We go through the various stages of shaping and building on the path of progress. Over time we strip away the excess that doesn't serve us. We are constantly improving, learning and overcoming challenges as we go through more stages of reshaping and rebuilding, being drawn along a path that is guided by who we feel we are.

There are times that we feel broken or bruised but, like the wood in my hands, I know that those parts can be reworked and strengthened, or appreciated as one part of our story. They add to the character and to the narrative.

At times, we can feel overworked and underappreciated, deflated and downtrodden. We need to recognise that in those moments, more than ever, we need to nurture ourselves — to sand out those knocks and scrapes, and apply another layer of protective oil.

The result of all our work will never be finished. We're not born finished and we certainly don't die finished. But the journey between the two points will be beautiful and of real value to this world. That's where the magic will be.

The physical object in which I see these parallels so clearly is that of the surfboard. When I think about making a surfboard, it's easy to get caught up in the seriousness of the process, the decisions and the practicality of it. Yet when all is said and done, the ultimate purpose is to use it to immerse yourself in the elements, feel the energy of the ocean, connect back to nature, to yourself, and enjoy the ride.

Play.

Laugh.

Share.

# YOU

# Welldoing

**To know even one life has breathed easier because you have lived. This is to have succeeded.**

— Ralph Waldo Emerson

When I first left the world of advertising to become a yoga teacher, I believed in the phrase, 'We are human beings not human doings'. In my new life, I was surrounded by people who believed in the power of now and the importance of wellbeing, and 'doing' had a bad name. As I felt the first rumblings of desire to do and create more, I felt confused. How could I do more, without compromising my wellbeing?

Over the last few years, as I have explored this inner conflict, I have come to realise that this battle is waged in the outside world too. It can appear as if there are two tribes: the *beings* who believe life is about who you are and how you feel, and the *doers* who believe life is about what you do and achieve.

Now I realise that they are the two sides of the same coin. There is *being* in *doing* and *doing* in *being*. In 2011, I called this integrated approach to life *welldoing*. It is at the heart of my personal life and my working life.

We are human beings *and* human doers.

*Welldoing* is not about balance — this assumes there is an ideal state of balance when in fact life is a myriad of moments in constant flux. *Welldoing* is about dynamic balance — the ability to ride the waves of life with skill and joy. The same subtle but important shift in understanding has happened in the world of medicine too. The concept of 'homeostasis' — when the body naturally looks for a state of balance — has been replaced by 'allostasis', meaning a state of dynamic balance. This is explained in Robert Sapolsky's classic book on stress, *Why Zebras Don't Get Ulcers*, as being about 'constancy through change'.

At night, by allowing the mind and body to follow a natural rhythm of light and deep sleep, we are recharged by dynamic balance.

During the day, by following periods of effort with ones of rest, we maintain higher energy levels through dynamic balance.

With every breath we take, by creating a smooth, regular and constant rhythm with our in and out breaths, we feel centred by dynamic balance.

Looking back at my life, there were a number of clues to these insights that I missed at the time but have discovered in researching my book. In a period of depression following the death of my brother, leading up to the new millennium, I was handed the book *You Can't Afford the Luxury of a Negative Thought* by John-Roger and Peter McWilliams. One of the chapters was about *being* and *doing* and the importance of both. I just wasn't ready to understand its significance back then, even if the authors admitted to including 'jokes stolen from coffee mugs' to make their point:

> **Some say, 'To do is to be.'**
> **Others say, 'To be is to do.'**
> **I tend to agree with Francis Albert Sinatra:**
> **'Do, be, do, be, do.'**

Later on, when I first picked up David Allen's *Getting Things Done*, which has been a major influence on how I get stuff done, I noticed it was dedicated to his spiritual coach J.R. — John-Roger, the co-author of *You Can't Afford*… So these worlds of being and doing merged — and that's where the magic is.

The most technologically advanced machine known is our own 'bodymind'. By harnessing the human body's natural mechanisms, we have an in-built ability to manage stress. Simply breathing well and in sync with your body's natural flow creates the foundation for you to reach your full potential. By organising yourself better and finding the courage to live outside of your comfort zone, you are transformed from 'worrier to warrior', as artist James Victore would say. Practising a more mindful life, can you appreciate the little things of life and savour the moment more.

**Every breath is a wave. Every heartbeat is a wave. Every thought is a wave. Every one of us is a wave.**

All the waves that rise and fall exist on the vast ocean of our lives. Yet at the same time, mindfulness and meditation take us down into the depths of that ocean. To a place of stillness, peace and inner calm.

Our doing and our being as one.

*Welldoing* is the synthesis of these contrasting experiences of life into one big dynamic whole. Embracing all that we experience and all that we offer with courage, skill and love.

To find inner calm and outer focus we all need to embrace a range of strategies and techniques that bring together how we are with what we do. Reducing your stress levels, improving your energy levels, focusing your mind and attention on what really matters to you; these can transform your life. By playing with these ideas and integrating them into your daily life I hope you too can find some magic and the passion to make it happen.

**Working hard for something we don't care about is called stress. Working hard for something we love is called passion.**

— Simon Sinek

## The 'bodymind'

Your body affects your mind and your mind affects your body. All too often, however, we listen to the neurotic ramblings of our mind and ignore the pleas of our bodies: 'please rest, please move, please eat ...' Once we start to listen and pay attention to our minds, our bodies and our breathing, we can really start to build strong foundations for a better day, and a better life.

## Breathe like a baby

Do you have a child? Do you remember watching them sleep as babies, their bellies naturally rising and falling? Do you remember their first breath? When I did a talk recently I introduced my breathing guru by showing a photo of a baby — because babies are the best breathers. Their minds and bodies are one. They breathe well because as human beings they are designed to. We can learn from them. Breathe from the belly, breathe through the nose. It's as simple as that. Who knows, it might also help you to sleep like a baby.

## How are you breathing now?

If breathing well is so natural, why do we lose the knack? When was the last time you stopped and noticed how you were breathing? Have you made the connection already between your breathing and how you feel? How about now? What do you observe? Are you breathing through your nose or your mouth? Can you feel your belly rising and falling? Or can you feel your chest lifting and expanding? Maybe you're even holding your breath?

The first step to improving how you breathe is awareness. Start to become more and more aware of how you breathe and how that changes under different conditions. Follow your own breath — it's your best teacher.

## The three keys to breathing well

There are many breathing exercises and techniques from both the East and the West. The basics, however, are simple.

1 **Breathe in and out from the belly.**
  Breathing from the belly you feel more centred and more in control. This diaphragmatic or abdominal breathing (I prefer to say 'belly') is efficient and, once established, easy and natural.

2 **Breathe in and out through the nose.**
  The nose is designed for breathing. The little hairs in the nostrils filter out particles in the air. The chamber behind the nose cools or warms the air to within one degree of the body's temperature. Except for certain situations like high-intensity sport, your nose does a much better job of breathing than your mouth.

3 **Breathe out a little more than you breathe in.**
  Exhaling is linked to the body's relaxation response as it stimulates the parasympathetic branch of the autonomic nervous system. Once you're in balance you can breathe in and out equally. But in my experience most of us are so frequently stressed that a little more exhalation with every breath is a good idea.

Words from *Do Breathe* by Michael Townsend Williams

Breathe in...

Breathe out...

# Breath and pause

Helene Simonsen is a classical musician. Since her instrument is the flute, there has to be pause in everything she plays, in order for her to breathe. For her, breathing is part of the music. Some composers signal where to pause and breathe, but with others (Bach in particular, she says) you have to find or make the space to pause for yourself. Pause is something that the musician, and the music, cannot do without. As Helene says, 'Whatever you are doing, if you want something else to happen, you need to pause.'

Without a pause, everything continues as it was. Even something as mechanical as changing gear in a car is smoother when you add the tiniest of pauses in neutral, between gears. Pausing is part of living and breathing. Indeed, between breathing in and breathing out, there's a pause. The purpose of having a break isn't only to rest, important though that may be. As Helene says, it allows something else to occur: 'my playing often develops through the breaks'. In a pause you can question existing ways of acting, have new ideas or simply appreciate the life you are living. Without ever stopping to observe yourself, how can you explore what else you might do or who you might become? If you always head on relentlessly, where is the room for the heart?

A life without pause is unhealthy, from the cellular level up. It profoundly affects how we feel. If you don't stop to think, life will force you to stop and think. At the extreme, the cost is 'burnout'.

It is a striking image, of being consumed by fire. These days burnout is increasingly common, especially among those people we think of and label as 'successful' — a fact that, surely, ought to give us pause for thought.

That isn't the only risk. When people burn out, it is crippling, but at least it is dramatic enough to demand attention. It forces reconsideration. Burnout can be seen as 'a sane reaction to an insane world', a response that comes from some buried inner wisdom, reasserting itself in a highly conspicuous way. Less extreme but more insidious is the slow, suffocating smoulder. As we constantly push on from one task to the next, we can become our to-do lists. Little by little, we learn to live with less of ourselves. It is death by a thousand meetings. What we could be becomes a forgotten dream.

As well as the cost to our health or sanity, there is the cost of what you miss along the way. Fail to pause and you miss out on the view, or the path not taken. What's more likely to get your kids to talk to you: questioning them or allowing them some space? With no pause (or silence) in a meeting, you may rattle through the agenda, but fail to tackle the underlying issues. What other more creative, more powerful conversations might you have, if only you were able to let a bit of daylight into the process? What deeper questions might be raised? What other voices might you hear? As you bowl along, are you really thinking or are you just reacting? Is packing more in really the way to do your best work, or to get the most out of life?

**We should take wandering outdoor walks, so that the mind might be nourished and refreshed by the open air and deep breathing.**

— Seneca

# ALL WALKING IS DISCOVERY. ON FOOT, WE TAKE THE TIME TO SEE THINGS WHOLE.

— Hal Borland

We walk for all kinds of reasons: to get groceries, go into town, travel to a friend's house, walk a dog, clear our heads or find inspiration. They all have value.

My MorningWalk — I refer to my daily practice of walking as 'MorningWalk' throughout this section — can be all that and something more. It has become a meditative practice, and therefore a bit different from simply 'going for a walk'. As with seated meditation, this practice mirrors the realities of life, the details of each day, changing and moving constantly. MorningWalk embraces connection, observation, movement and constant change. It has become my paradigm for a way of being in the world, in harmony with the way the natural world operates.

Walking is rather narrowly understood, but it has the potential to be life changing. To understand it as life changing requires a clarity of intention, surrender of destination, dedication to the moment and commitment to a practice. Your MorningWalk may not look like my MorningWalk, and that is wonderful. It may be in an urban neighbourhood or a rural community; it may include wheels; it may include a furry companion, or not. No matter where or how you go, there you are: committed to a practice, open to the moment and embracing the ever-changing circumstances.

Come, join me on a MorningWalk.

# Walk as if you are kissing the earth with your feet.

— Thich Nhat Hanh

It is 5.02 am, a Tuesday morning in September 2020; the cool air is beginning to replace the slow, humid, heavy air of summer. It is noticeably darker at this time in the morning than it was a week ago. I must admit there is a lovely anticipation of the coming autumn months but also a hint of dread as the deep cold of a New England winter is just weeks away. Changing seasons make the world feel hopeful, familiar and promising. They are a powerful reminder that change is the natural state of affairs. These inevitable shifts can bring with them a beautiful feeling of newness and also the feeling that nothing is stable. Walking in every distinct and unique season has been a series of glorious and unyielding lessons. An ongoing lesson in transformation, in embracing all that is in each unique moment.

Every morning when I pull on my shoes and head out the door, I am inspired by how walking every damn day has fundamentally changed my life. There are the obvious shifts in fitness level, increased appetite, better sleep and more perspective, but the subtle shifts are perhaps where the magic resides. My sense of time has changed. My understanding of distance has forever been re-modelled. Step by singular step, I have walked over 25,000 miles, enough miles to circumnavigate the earth. This has taken me nine years. I no longer think of this as 'just a morning walk'. I now call it 'my MorningWalk', a sacred act to start the day. This, however, wasn't always the case.

When I first committed to going for a walk every day, I had to get over my athletic ego. I had spent much of my life defined as 'an athlete'. During my high-school years I played field hockey, basketball and lacrosse and, by my senior year, I was captain of all three teams. In college I started rowing, and did that for four years, including competing in the National Championships. For decades, my self-worth came from how well I played. So, when I started to … walk … it took me, in truth, a year or two to get comfortable with something so low key. I would eventually come to understand that MorningWalk wasn't an athletic endeavour: it was something else.

Looking back, I can see that MorningWalk has been a serendipitous pilgrimage of sorts. A surprising journey, a daily adventure: cold, hot, sunny, rainy, boring, exciting, joyous, heavy, creative, innovative and loving. When I started I didn't know the profound impact it would have on my life. In fact, at the time it felt like a small gesture, a simple dedication of some time to get outside and go for a walk. After nine years of walking every day it has become an essential practice that feels like devotion — perhaps even prayer.

The important thing has not been the mileage or how fast; in fact, I am very aware that many have run/walked/biked/hiked/rolled 25,000+ miles in a much shorter time frame, or perhaps have had a similar practice for many more years than I. If you are an avid runner then undoubtedly you have already covered these miles over the course of your life. I have friends and colleagues who I think of as The Original Walkers; I think some of them have had a MorningWalk practice for several decades and likely have walked the distance to the moon and back.

No, MorningWalk isn't about how many miles or how many years — although those are markers of a sort — instead it is about the loyalty and enthusiasm for each walk. It became a subtle practice that saved me. It saved my spirit. It saved my way of being. Ultimately, it reminded me who I am.

# If one just keeps on walking, everything will be all right.

— Søren Kierkegaard

This isn't about walking as an act of redemption — it is about a slow, natural realisation that there is great joy that can come from a wildly simple change and commitment in your life. MorningWalk is a micro daily habit that has the potential of having a macro lifelong impact. It is a gentle, slow practice ... and pace (not speed) matters. There is no rushing, no urgency embedded into a step. It isn't a task to 'get over' so I can move on to the next thing on the list. Instead it is an opportunity to be aligned with the pace of the natural world. I had lost touch with that. My days had become to-do lists and looking at the clock to get to the next thing on time.

In fact, when I look to the natural world the only things that move quickly, with urgency and speed, are things that are often destructive: nor'easters, earthquakes, hurricanes, wildfires. Life was moving too quickly. There was too much untethered energy. Walking was a way back to a pace that was natural and recognisable, and also a way to truly be open, to see what each day was going to bring. Mama Nature has her own pace and the 21st-century world has a different energy and pace that felt out of alignment to me. The 'normal' societal pace meant that I had forgotten we are part of the natural world, with a need to slow down before we can really understand, know and hear what we need.

MorningWalk has become a way of life. It is a subtle, cumulative, spiritual, physical, creative, healing, unhurried, essential practice that has required discipline, commitment and a splash of wild optimism to make it profoundly impactful. Walking is what makes us human. To go for a walk is perhaps one of the most primal things we do each day. A dear friend, Eric, when asked how he was, would always answer: 'I'm fine. I am walking the earth.' Walking the earth has been a way to ground myself, to centre myself, to find the heartbeat both in myself and of a place, a road, a path, a walkway, a sidewalk, a field....

Small rituals can be a joyous way to kickstart the day and at the same time provide powerful comfort. A walk, a cup of tea, breath work, making the bed, morning pages. I knew a daily ritual had the potential to be a tool to engage my mind, a way to clear the trash out of my head, a daily dose of beauty and physical satisfaction, an ongoing source of humility and a generous wellspring of contentment in the certainty of it; but I didn't realise until years into this practice how essential it would become.

## SATURDAY, 13 FEBRUARY 2016

*What a glorious morning. Cold, bright, hopeful, and feeling
grateful. I started this practice because I needed to get back
to a bigger sense of purpose and clarity, one that began with a
fundamental intimacy with the earth. On this morning, I have
seen the sun come up, a coyote, several blue jays, an eagle, and
the start to my 54th year. I have come to realise that making a
commitment and following through with it is what love looks
like. This hasn't been an easy path these last five years or so,
but I haven't missed a day. Some walks have felt impossible.
Yet every walk has been a gift. An opportunity to add energy,
focus and space to the day. Space to hold overwhelming
thoughts, to hear essential intuition, to toss around silly ideas,
to look at gut reactions, to play with messy concepts, to feel
grateful and to celebrate another pass around the sun.
Happy birthday to me.*

## FRIDAY, 8 JUNE 2018

*Our advertising agency has a big presentation to an important
client in a week and we are still working to get to the right idea.
As creative director, one of the most terrifying elements of
my job is I'm never quite sure when or where The Idea or
The Solution may show up. As the days pass, the tension,
anxiety and excitement build. There is a complexity to this
moment when we start assessing ideas with the team and my
feedback goes something like this:*

> *'Interesting idea, but not quite there yet.'*
> *'Nope.'*
> *'Love it, keep going.'*
> *'Bananas.'*
> *'Great start, however ...'*
> *'Wonderful, but no.'*
> *'Maybe.'*
> *'It's a beginning.'*
> *'That's crazy, good concept.'*

*We were getting nowhere fast so I put on my walking shoes
and invited my colleagues to join me. I wanted to inspire a
collision of conversation and observations, and to unearth
and unlock new ways of thinking. I also wanted us to be on
an equal footing. No one sat at the head of the table in this
meeting. Hierarchy didn't matter. We were aligned and equal
in our commitment to find a great idea as we walked through
the town.*

## FRIDAY, 23 AUGUST 2019

*I received some news that was very difficult. Life-alteringly, intimately difficult. The ultimate betrayal. As I left the office that afternoon, I told myself that I could either go home and curl up in bed to try and feel better, or, I could walk. I went home, put on my shoes and set out to do my familiar loop of 7.3 miles. I walked through the night. All. Night. Step by painful step. I needed to keep walking.*

*Each lap held a different emotion. There was big anger, wild frustration, bold denial, pure rage, broken trust — sometimes all at once. Each lap became an elegant chapter about grieving, about reflection, about pain, about finding my way back to myself. I stayed out until sunrise, went home, took a shower and walked to work.*

## SATURDAY, 2 JANUARY 2021

*Good morning, New Year. Just returned from a very, very
long and beautiful walk. Twelve miles, about three hours.
It was gorgeous. Bright. Calm. Cold. It all felt so hopeful and
nourishing. I didn't want to come in. I wanted to breathe in
the sunlight and the birdsong. I used the space around me
to discard the negative voices in my head from last year.
Left along the side of the road are all those distracting
unhelpful thoughts that worked their way into my mind:
'You aren't — enough.' 'You are too —.' 'Why did you say —?'
Blah, blah, blah. As I walk it is easier and easier to leave these
stories behind and what remains? A brilliant, sparkly day,
abundant with accompanying gratitude.*

*Walk. Breathe in. Breathe out.
Notice everything. Notice this day.*

*Halfway through today's walk I came upon a snowy owl —
a rare sight and a pure pleasure. In the past, I would have
missed it. Life can be so busy we overlook what is right in front
of us. Today is different. Years of practice have taught me to
slow down and look up. As I walked past the snowy owl, she
took off, circled around and landed just up the road, almost
as if to say, 'Come on, keep going.'*

**The journey of a thousand miles begins with one step.**

— Lao Tzu

# REGENERATE

# Earth consciousness

I spent my twenties scared of climate disaster and busy organising. In my early thirties I burnt out from living with zero balance and too much activism. I'd made it my mission to stop climate change. When I realised that heaping it all on me wasn't just impossible but also delusional, I felt like I'd failed at the only thing that gave my life meaning.

Since then, I've been slowly putting myself back together and in the process re-evaluating my relationship to activism and to the planet I've been so desperate to 'save'.

It's a funny idea that we who have caused nature so much harm will be the ones to save the planet. It's an idea that makes human success or failure the centre of the story, when we might learn more if we became humble and focused our attention on the earth's strength and resilience. We got into this mess because we dominated nature, forcing it to provide our every consumer want. Instead of showing care and respect, we extracted until we reached this point of environmental crisis.

We have pushed both our planet and ourselves, ignoring natural limits. Instead of learning from the earth about how to rest, heal and regenerate, we celebrate humankind as separate from and dominating nature. I want to let go of such an arrogant worldview. I want to give up trying to control the natural world and other humans too. Fighting bad policies is part of a new story that is taking root, but to heal we don't just need to fight, we also need to become enchanted by the planet again.

The way nature brings peace to my busy mind feels like one of the most abandoned parts of who I am. Slowly I am rekindling it. I walk in the woods and I feel at ease. It becomes easy to hear the world whisper, 'This is everything that is happening right now.' Lost beneath the boughs of trees, there's nothing I need and instead I feel healing power between the earth and me.

I read articles about people who talk to plants. Their mental health improves and the data shows their plants grow stronger. I pay attention when I catch sight of a jay's turquoise feather or a blue tit's yellow chest and it feels like a gift. Walking through a forest on a winter's day, the sunlight reflects through tiny droplets of caught, cold water and transforms my path into a lair of delicate jewels. I delight in these things the more that I realise I'm part of them. At an atomic level I belong to nature and Earth's nourishment is written into the coils of my DNA.

This story of belonging with nature is the one I want to return to all my life. It's the beginning of a more sophisticated environmental practice than just loudly saying no. We will still need to turn away from the fossil-fuel era, but when we look to nature's abundance we can feel inspired about what the next phase of human evolution might be.

# Building foundations

For anything to last, it needs strong foundations. For a business to continue giving value to the world, we must explore its life-giving properties. In order to do so, we need to move beyond the idea of sustainability to the idea of regeneration. One way for business to do good is by regenerating our economy, our environment and our civilisation. The foundations of business now and in the future must be premised on regeneration, creating the conditions for all of life to thrive. For me, these foundations must include beauty, nature, biomimicry, design, values and metrics, and governance.

## Beauty

The human spirit needs beauty. It enriches us and lifts us up. Beauty is a felt knowledge, connecting us spiritually, intellectually, sensually and ethically to every part of our lives. It expresses the idea that we can seek the good and manifest it in all that we create in this world. What I have learned since writing *Do Design* is that the human spirit strives for more beauty. Beauty is good; it is a universal truth that beauty is a vital part of our DNA. Beautiful things are prepared with love and infused with optimism. They simply say life is, and can be, worthwhile. But how can beauty be a frame for business?

Peter Childs, who was the founding Head of the Dyson School of Design Engineering at Imperial College London, says beauty should be reclaimed by schools teaching business. He believes beauty offers a different way of framing our world: 'We talk about rationale, philosophies, aesthetics and ascetics. The concept of beauty tends to be reserved for the beauties of nature. Can we actually set out to do something beautiful? There is an aspiration worthy of aiming towards. Can we teach beautiful design, beautiful engineering? It is probably a bit like, can we teach subjects such as creativity?'

Childs goes on: 'Well, we can certainly augment creativity, and beauty would be a subject where one could augment and enhance what people are already doing, and I suspect with time actually lift the whole cohort, so that what they are doing in terms of their impact on society could truly be beautiful.'

In essence, beauty is a verb, 'I do.' It should be our frame for life.

Climeworks is an exemplar of Childs's suggestion that there is a cohort motivated to make a positive contribution to our world. Climate change is both a challenge and an opportunity. Ten billion tons of carbon dioxide needs to be removed from the air every year and stored. Simple maths, just a really big number. Climeworks technology extracts carbon dioxide directly from the atmosphere, and uses it to provide renewable energy or make carbonated beverages, or turns it into stone and stores it deep underground. The technology is pioneering and their business enables individuals as well as organisations to contribute to climate take back and carbon dioxide reduction through a subscription model. This is regenerative economics in practice.

Everlane also belongs to this cohort that is striving to find innovative ways of restoring equilibrium between our economy, our ecology and our community. The company sells sustainably sourced clothing. Founded in 2011, it has 1.5 million customers. 'Clothes should be built to last,' says the CEO of Everlane, Michael Preysman. 'The question for all other leaders out there is, what side of history do you want to be on? We have a belief you can be ethical and profitable.' The denim factory that makes its jeans recycles 98 per cent of its water.

## Nature

Nature is calling us, because we are part of nature. We belong to the natural world, because we are made from the same molecular material. This is not a romantic notion; there is evidence that demonstrates our relationship with nature is fundamental to our mental health and spiritual wellbeing — green spaces bring health benefits, for example. So, why wouldn't you protect the very thing from which you are made? According to Buddhist philosophy, our true nature is to be caring and kind. We need to see the bigger picture.

When introducing people to the beauty of nature, I ask them to shut their eyes and visualise themselves in a spaceship. Looking out of a window, they can see the sun, the earth and the moon, hanging in the endless void. Sitting next to them is the astronaut Edgar Mitchell, and he is saying that when he first saw our planet and the celestial bodies from space, he was overcome by a sense of wonder or euphoria that flowed through his body.

I ask them to imagine that Mitchell looks at them and says the molecules in his body and the molecules in this spaceship and in their body are all forged in an ancient star: 'We are all stardust.' I go on to tell a story of how astronauts experience the 'Overview' effect. This is a cognitive shift where they are motivated by a deep need to protect the earth and serve humanity. They realise there are no borders, and we are one species. That earth is a tiny fragile planet, existing in the vast infinite entity that is space.

I ask people to open their eyes. Resistance has dissipated. Instead, there is a pathway for me to speak about the joy that the natural world gives us, how it can foster wonder and why we know we belong to its pure state.

I then ask this question: If we are all made of the same stuff, what is our role in this world and how do we act? This exercise is one I have delivered many times. To begin with, it is greeted with varying degrees of scepticism. But it is a means to reconnect people to nature. It is a way to reframe and understand our connection with the natural world, without which we can neither respect nor wish to protect our fragile earth.

Seeing the world as deeply interconnected is imperative, for the simple reason of understanding cause and effect. Since we are entangled in creation, it is vital for us to show care and respect for what we have. Without this deep reframing, we may struggle to meet design challenges and be less willing to seek transformative solutions to problems of manufacturing, architecture and resources. We could be less inclined to make creative leaps of the imagination in developing the products and services that this world needs.

## Biomimicry

Nature is running one of the longest and most continuous Research and Development projects around. No company could ever afford such a long-term investigation into what makes life thrive. Moreover, nature works on the principle of regeneration, with a complex ecosystem that supports all of life. It makes sense to learn from the gift of nature, as it offers a way of understanding the limits of growth and how to share resources. It is here that business can draw inspiration from nature's principles.

Biomimicry is the practice of learning how the natural world designs itself, and applying that knowledge to how we farm, produce energy, manufacture products, heal ourselves and build things. In her book *Biomimicry: Innovation Inspired by Nature*, the natural sciences writer Janine Benyus describes nature's principles: nature runs on sunlight, uses only the energy it needs, fits form to function, recycles everything, rewards co-operation, banks diversity, demands local expertise, curbs excesses and taps the power of limits. These principles point us towards a productive way of thinking about business, as a philosophy and a practice. In doing so, they form the basis of questions about how a business could operate, and enable a reimagining and resetting of the benchmark of what it means to be in business.

Forward-facing companies use principles of biomimicry in their design, engineering, supply chains and business models. Consider the flooring manufacturer Interface, which set itself a goal to transform its business model to become climate-positive by working on carbon-negative products. This was a long journey, but its story is important as it shows that even an established company can embark on transformation.

Geanne van Arkel, the Head of Sustainable Development EMEA (Europe, Middle East and Africa) at Interface, says, 'We have no choice if we want to be in business in the medium and long term. We have raised the bar, and our goal now is to become a company that is regenerative. This is what everyone should want, otherwise there is no beauty in the things you do — be it living, working or doing business.'

As another example, look at Bolt Threads, which produces two innovative materials using production processes inspired by nature: Microsilk, inspired by the properties of spider silk, and Mylo, a leather material made from mycelium, part of a fungus. The manufacturing of textiles is the second-largest source of pollution on the planet. Bolt's materials are produced with less waste and fewer natural resources to reduce this environmental impact. Bolt envisions a world where we don't have to deplete or pollute our forests, oceans and rivers to benefit from their natural secrets. What if better days for our planet lie ahead?

# Regenerating our world

Our responsibility is also to ensure we create ways in which we can measure the return to equilibrium between our economy, our ecology and our community. Equilibrium demands we address scale and growth. We must design businesses for scale as nature intended, rather than for infinite growth. Think about how water flows from a source, from a spring to a river and an estuary to an ocean — all are connected, all are needed. Growth needs to be circular, and reciprocal.

If by scaling we take more than we are able to replace, or we create suffering, then we should not be forcing the scaling of the business. If we are to grow, then it should be done so that growth feels inevitable and continues to create abundance in the world. Does the world need us, and does the world need more of us?

## Leading with generosity

In regenerating our world, we need leadership to be rooted in wisdom. This is leadership steeped in values with the desire to be a good ancestor. Your work, to create a legacy for future generations, is your gift to the world. Approaching leadership with a sense of generosity is the way forward. This is about knowing how to nurture joyful working cultures and building a place where people love the work they do. Beautiful things can only ever be made with love.

A beautiful leader takes full responsibility for themselves, developing their own practice to restore and regenerate the economy and the environment. Otherwise, how could you lead with generosity, compassion and empathy?

## The telling of stories

Leadership requires you to be a powerful storyteller, firing people's imaginations and inviting others to draw from the deepest wells of their creativity. Make no mistake, words create worlds; language is generative. Stories have potency, describing how we can be in the world. We can see what stories visualise and the ideas they contain. From a story perspective, if we cannot describe a new destination that excites, motivates and evokes a yearning in people, we will never get there.

Consider the climate crisis: we are all doomed. How do you feel? Excited, motivated, ready to give your all to the task ahead? Unlikely. But what if we think about climate change as an opportunity, offering the means to rethink, redesign and remake our world? Some might describe this as utopian, but we don't get to create or discover anything without belief and optimism, even under the most perilous conditions.

Enduring stories carry an irreducible truth and symbolism, standing impervious to time. Narratives call us to listen. They shape our beliefs. The stories we tell now must describe our quest for regeneration. If our stories fail to inspire who we want to become, then we fail too. But when we do succeed, our best stories inspire a desire for a better world, generating the capacity to make great things that transcend generations, even centuries.

There are certain pursuits which,
if not wholly poetic and true,
do at least suggest a nobler and finer
relation to nature than we know.
The keeping of bees, for instance.

— Henry David Thoreau

# How to fall in love with the Earth

When we're ready to learn, nature will teach us everything we need to know about how to relate to each other, the earth and ourselves. When we're ready, the earth will show us how to heal.

Dying nature creates new ecosystems. Dead trees provide habitat, cycle nutrients, regenerate plants, capture carbon and keep soil wet. Nature is abundant and the different elements within it create a dance of balance and reciprocity. When nature is in charge, everything is what it is and exactly what it should be.

However hard we try to think our way out of it, we are natural creatures too. We rebel against this, burdened as we are with fretful brains. Collectively we have exerted our power to dominate everything, including our earth.

There is much for us to relearn and remember from nature. Even in these times, the earth is so rich. If we were to stop waste, celebrate generosity and condemn greed, we can imagine a world of plenty. It's not so far away. The biggest step to getting there will be when we stop trying to bend nature to our fears of scarcity and instead open ourselves up to her patterns of abundance.

## Take the long view

We're stuck in habits that have started to feel like dead-ends. Nature blows a way through and leads us to age-old healing practices like the acceptance of change, curiosity, interdependence, resilience and patience. We can all be more like the bulb in winter, accepting and respecting the seasons and trusting that new and beautiful life will come.

We can look to the earth and to the people who have not severed their intelligence from the earth's wisdom. Indigenous people have been stewards of the planet for thousands of years. According to a *National Geographic* article, they make up less than 5 per cent of the global population and yet the land they dwell on supports more than 80 per cent of global biodiversity. Where Indigenous people have been living, nature has continued to thrive. We should be listening to their philosophies and amplifying them throughout all our cultures, whether in urban or rural settings. We need to learn from Indigenous people to stop assaulting biodiversity and to re-establish a reciprocal relationship with our planet.

One of the most widely repeated Native American philosophies is the seventh-generation principle. It's based on the Haudenosaunee (Iroquois) Great Law of Peace (Gayanashagowa). The principle states that we should make decisions about how we live today based on how our decisions will impact the next seven generations to come. If we can make practical this principle, we will be good caretakers of the earth, not simply for ourselves, but for those who will inherit the earth and the results of our decisions.

Seven generations is around 140 years away. Between now and then there will be countless decisions made by countless people all trying to secure a life worth living. The purpose of all these lives will change as new pressures take hold and old pressures are released. It's going to take some careful retuning to orient our lives to care for such future descendants and to learn from people whose ways are channels of earth consciousness.

# SUSTAIN

# STAYING IN THE HOUSE BREEDS A SORT OF INSANITY, ALWAYS.

— Henry David Thoreau

I notice first a wisp of smoke rising above the horizon.
As I approach, I hear the sound of laughter and, closer
still, the crack and pop of a wood fire. It's the smell
though, a warm smokiness mingled with something
savoury bubbling in a pot, that draws me in.

Kneeling down, I poke the fire with a stick and stir
the pot. It's satisfying and I breathe out. I catch the eye
of the others and we begin to talk more freely; it feels
good to be known.

A taste of the wild, an ancient thing, a good thing
indeed. We know what it is to be truly alive.

**SUSTAIN**

## Ingredients

1 cup spelt or barley grains
1 cup lentils (any type)
Generous glug of oil
1 cinnamon stick
1 tbsp cumin seeds
1 tbsp coriander seeds
4 onions (2 red, 2 white is good), chopped
½ head of garlic, cloves smashed
3 red peppers, deseeded and roughly chopped
1 green pepper, deseeded and roughly chopped
2 × 400g tins chopped tomatoes
1 × 400g tin kidney beans, drained and sieve-rinsed
2 whole Scotch bonnet chillies (or similar)
1 cup strong black coffee
Big squeeze of tomato purée
3 tbsp muscovado sugar
½ bar dark chocolate (I would say a whole bar, but I usually end up eating half)
Salt and pepper
Big handful of fresh coriander
Soured cream, to serve

# Vegetarian *'I can't believe there's no meat, this is amazing!'* Chilli

*When we go on a family camping trip, more often than not, we'll make a big chilli the day before, take it with us on the journey and heat it up as we're setting up camp. The great thing about veggie chilli is that it's all low-risk foods (no meat), and most people can eat it. It's a relatively cheap and calorific meal for the hungry ones, and on a cooler night, this raises the bar in terms of comfort food. Also the non-perishable nature of the ingredients makes this chilli an ideal end-of-trip meal, as the ingredients don't need to be kept cool. Warning: contains beans. Lash those wind flaps.*

**Makes:** enough for 6
**Takes:** 30 minutes' prep, plus a couple of hours' slow cooking (but longer is better)
**Fire:** low and slow friendly fire
**Kit:** chopping board, sharp knife, sieve, Dutch oven or large heavy pan with a lid, metal tongs, wooden spoon, large bowl, a tripod for hanging your pot above the fire would be ideal

## Method

Soak your grains and lentils in 2 cups of water — the longer the better. Meanwhile, set your Dutch oven up over a low-medium heat and add the oil and whole spices. Add the chopped onions and, once they are golden, add the smashed garlic. Add the peppers and allow to soften for 5 minutes, stirring occasionally to see nothing burns to the bottom (add a dash more oil if things are sticking).

Now add the tinned tomatoes and drained and rinsed beans. Swill the tomato tins out with water and add this to the chilli too. Add all the remaining ingredients (except the coriander), including the grains and lentils and their starchy water. Stir the whole lot together and pop the lid on.

Drink any spare coffee (cook's bonus). Stir the chilli occasionally, checking for seasoning and chilli heat and making sure it doesn't catch on the bottom (top up with more water if needed).

After about 1 hour, your chilli should be lovely and thick — once the grains are soft with a little bite, the chilli is done. You know how you like your chilli.

Stir in the chopped coriander and serve with a big dollop of soured cream. It's also ace with a smashed avocado and goes really well with cornbread or baked potatoes.

## Tips

— Add the Scotch bonnet chilies to the pot whole. Periodically taste your chilli — when the heat level is just right you can whip these out.

— For a lovely extra depth of sweet smoky flavour, grill your peppers first directly on the embers, turning them occasionally with metal tongs. Once the skin is charred and black all over, allow them to cool in a large bowl covered with clingfilm. After 5–10 minutes, the charred skins will easily slip off. Deseed and proceed.

— A favourite in our house is cheapie tortilla wraps, cut into big triangles and fried in some oil until crispy. These are then used as a tasty spade to shovel the chilli into your cake hole. Spud skins are also ideal.

— Make this at home, freeze and take it with you frozen. It'll keep your other perishable ingredients cool as it defrosts.

— This pot gets better with time, so if you want to make the most of spending time with the people you're with, make this the day before. And come hungry o'clock, simply heat and serve. Faff-free wild cooking.

# Wild baking shortcuts

**Ain't got much time? Ain't got no skills?**
Try any of these quickie recipes for some naked fire cooking:

### Mussels
Take a bag with you and just throw individual mussels on hot embers. Remove with tongs and add a squeeze of lemon.

### Spuds
Toss potatoes deep into the fire, cover with embers and leave for an hour. Melted butter + cheese = feast.

### Corn on the cob
Leave all the leaves on and push under the embers for 15 minutes. Butter, salt, nibble, nibble.

### S'mores
Toast giant marshmallows until golden, then sandwich between chocolate biscuits. Come on!

### Popcorn
Put corn in a baggy foil parcel, drop on the fire — you'll hear when it's done.

# How to spark a conversation

*I used to have a mug with conversation starters on it that was made by my friend, Alice Hodge. It was always a good talking point and it struck me that my book,* Do Wild Baking, *could serve a similar purpose. An opportunity to open up conversations beyond the recipe. So I put a post on social media and these are a few of the responses (thank you!), plus a few of my own. And some from the mug.*

— Do you want a drink?
— Where did you grow up?
— What's your favourite smell?
— Would you rather be a bird or a fish?
— What have you watched lately that you enjoyed?
— What in your life gives you a sense of purpose?
— What are you committed to?
— What are you passionate about?
— What was the last thing your heart was really on fire for, and when was that?
— If you could travel to any place, from any period of time, where would you go, with whom, and why?
— What would your last supper be, where would you have it and with whom (dead or alive)?
— What would you do if you had no fear?
— What would you do if you knew you couldn't fail?
— What does the future look like if things go your way?
— If you could live your life again, what would you do differently from what you have done? ('Nothing' is not acceptable.)
— If you won the lottery, what would you do?
— If you knew you were going to die in 5 years, or 6 months, what would you do with the time?
— If your life were a book, how would your story go and would it be a bestseller?
— If you could write the eulogy for your funeral, what would it say?
— Another drink?
— Are you happy?
— What shall we have for breakfast?

**INSTRUCTIONS FOR LIVING A LIFE: PAY ATTENTION. BE ASTONISHED. TELL ABOUT IT.**

— Mary Oliver

# Coming home

We love coming home. We love the welcoming nature of thoughtfulness, intention and, of course, great style. We love having well-worn spots where our shoes, dog leads and bags routinely sit. The weight of the day comes off alongside our belongings.
We catch a glimpse of a framed photobooth strip hung on the wall, of a lichen-covered stick from a walk last weekend set on the coffee table, of air plants dressing the windowsill. We let familiarity find its way in and feel the wave of reassurance and gratitude for a space we've created that perfectly suits us. We find great comfort in knowing which corner is our favourite to curl up in. A space that is ours, where we feel at ease.

Our space and style are an extension of who we are. You can learn so much about a person when you walk into their home. You see character, personality and practicality intertwine.
We are intricately tied to the spaces we inhabit. They affect us — and those around us. They change how we move through our everyday life. Styling a space begins with how we want to live in it and, in essence, how we want to live.

Home is where we put down roots and connect — to ourselves and our families, partners, even our animals. It is a space to rejuvenate and grow. A shelter for what and who we love.
A place for our collections — the objects we pick up along the way that weave a tapestry of our stories and memories.

Surrounding yourself with things that bring you joy, and that ground you, creates a sense and a space that invite serenity and awareness. We must make space for our senses to come alive — and come to rest. Addresses change and tastes evolve, but our homes should always be a sanctuary.

You may live in a barn, a cabin, a city apartment, or even a boat. There is no size restriction to how a space can feel. Creativity and attention don't end with your personal space, but it's a good place to start. Create a space that contains the things you need to think more freely and express yourself openly. Where you can relax, meditate, entertain, read and work. Wellbeing starts where you sleep, eat and live. This is our guide to help you create such a place.

Less noise, more Earth; less house, more home.

# Study nature, love nature, stay close to nature. It will never fail you.

— Frank Lloyd Wright

Bringing the outside in is at the core of our design style. Not simply because it's beautiful, or can introduce great texture and tones, but because it keeps us grounded and connected to the Earth. Surrounding ourselves and designing with beauty from the outdoors makes us happier, healthier and calmer. Noticing the colours, structure and growth of flora and incorporating that into our spaces can cultivate more than just creativity. It can cultivate style.

It may not be for everyone, but our style stems from nature. We love finding feathers, stones and shells. We can't stop putting seed pods in vessels and branches on shelves, or hanging sticks from ceilings and walls. We make lighting from fallen birch trees and tree roots. Tree stumps serve as our end tables and double as perfect solutions for outdoor seating. We style every space with the love of nature in mind. It is truly a wild habit. We work to incorporate nature into a space, but not overwhelm it. We are continually inspired by being outside and finding ways to design products and spaces that reflect that.

# This is the first, the wildest and the wisest thing I know: that the soul exists and is built entirely out of attentiveness.

— Mary Oliver

Details may be perceived as small, but they are a large part of what makes your house a home. When styled well, it is the details that make a significant statement, that make your space unique. They will define it. Details are what will spark a memory or make a difference. It's what people respond to and remember.

Details don't just begin and end with well-chosen artwork or design elements. It is everything in between. It comes from *prutsen* — messing around. It's the how and the why. When you start to look at every part of an object — and each room as an opportunity for beauty — your space will start to feel full and even necessary. It's the joy you find in the small ring dish you have by the sink given to you by your best friend, or your grandfather's wooden screwdriver in your tool drawer. It isn't just a stack of books; it's the choice of books you love and want to showcase, and the feather bookmark you use to save your place.

Such details hold sentiment and stories. These are the things that will fill your space, that will draw you in and keep you still. When you style with purpose, with a raison d'être, you are putting more consideration into your home and into your life. Paying attention is inherently creative. You are giving your things a sense of belonging and a place to belong.

**Danielle:** I have a stick that has travelled with me everywhere I've lived. It is a walking stick my dad carved while camping over twenty years ago. It is plain, mostly straight, and isn't of much note other than it hangs on a wall. It doesn't have any intricate detail or even make much of a statement, but it has been the centrepiece of my home for as long as I can remember. Just as his memory that lives in it is most certainly the centrepiece of my life. This is detail, the things that not only add to the atmosphere of your home but to the sentiment of your life.

**Sue:** I have a hand-forged feather that sits on my desk. I remember so clearly the blacksmith who made it and the moments between it being made and being handed to me. I'm transported back in time to that day. It reminds me of kindness. It's most often these small details and objects that bring me the greatest joy and elicit the sweetest memories. These are the things and the feelings I take note of when I step into someone else's space. It makes paying attention so worthwhile.

Much like a handwritten note, when you take the extra time and extra effort to style your spaces, it doesn't go unnoticed. By determining what is necessary, what pieces you enjoy and prioritising what matters, you give your home and your objects room to shine and breathe.

# At some point in life, the world's beauty becomes enough.

— Toni Morrison

As you look around, you should start to see stories emerge from every shelf and consideration peek from every corner. Your style should start to feel intentional. Consideration and creativity are hopefully becoming dominant features of your space.

Beauty is a great igniter. To be better, try harder, look further. As you inhabit your space and style it in a way that reflects who you are and who you want to be, remember you too are ever evolving. Your home is a gathering place to nurture growth, ideas, change and beauty. It exists to foster relationships and creativity. It's meant to nourish, replenish, protect. It is a collective of moments, stories and artefacts.

Paying attention to what you seek, to what catches your eye and to what makes you happy are all the steps to a fuller life. If you always remember to keep looking and keep trying, your home will undoubtedly reflect your efforts. Living a creative and considered life starts with paying attention and with caring.

When each corner of your home has been considered, it will inevitably spread into the corners of your life. At the centre of making a beautiful space, style is often what is missing. As you find your style, consider what is missing and fill your spaces with things that are meaningful to you, we hope you find joy and gratitude for all the beauty you are bringing in. Style, like most things, comes with practice. Keep practising. Be patient. Pay attention. *Prutsen*.

# Waste not, want not

A shocking fact was revealed by government-sponsored research quite recently: upwards of 30 per cent of UK bread is thrown away uneaten, much of it still in its wrapper.

Whatever this sad statistic tells us about the connection between low price and low esteem in industrial baking, part of the problem may stem from skewed perceptions of freshness and a cultural aversion to ageing. Almost all industrial loaves are laced with synthetic enzymes to keep them soft for days or weeks. If every slice is identically 'fresh', the only way of divining its real age is by consulting the 'use by' label. Thus trust in our own sensory experience is undermined by the dictatorship of dates and an irrational fear of putrefaction.

In contrast, the sourdough baker embraces the passing of time as an indispensable contributor to the quality of, and our delight in, bread.

Without time, sourdough fermentation has no meaning. And I would argue that our pleasure in baked bread is one-dimensional (if not illusory) if it excludes any part of a loaf's passage from newly baked to stale.

Even sourdough starters, which have a habit of accumulating and threatening to outgrow their containers, are far from a 'waste' product. So never throw any surplus away, but use it (no matter how old and sour) in small quantities — up to 10 per cent — in almost any yeasted bread, where acid by-products will both flavour and strengthen the dough, and very likely keep it moister for longer.

It's all a matter of definition. If we get the bread right, it simply cannot be wasted, because it is useful and enjoyable throughout its life. And what could be more relevant to modern lives? If we're really too busy to bake and rushing to the shops isn't an option, let's make the best of what's left.

Here, as a celebration of time's benign role in sourdough baking, I propose 'The Seven Days of Bread'. See how the gradual mellowing of a baked loaf suggests a week of different and delicious uses.

As soon as it is baked and cooled, the process of 'staling' begins. Slowly, the starches harden and the moist crumb dries out. In sourdough breads, the flavour becomes more pronounced and 'mature'. With each change comes a new adaptation to what the bread can offer.

These, of course, are mere suggestions — and fairly obvious ones at that. I'm sure you will come up with more and better ideas.

# THE SEVEN DAYS OF BREAD

### DAY 1

## Fresh

Just out of the oven. No butter (but some self-control) needed. Perfect.

# Sandwich

Still soft, but firm enough to hold a filling.

# Toast

Drying out. Toasting both crisps the outside of the bread and softens the starches of the inner layer of the slice (unless you go on too long). Best eaten just warm, not hot.

# Bruschetta

Getting quite dry, but not 'stale'. Toast lightly, top with peppers, onions, olives, goats' cheese, etc., and finish under the grill.

# Crisp breads

Drier still. Slice very thinly with a good bread knife, lay out on a baking tray and dry out in a very low oven until completely crisp. This is great for sourdough breads that have turned out a bit flat or misshapen.

## DAY 6

# Croutons

Hard tack. Slice into 1.5cm (0.5in) cubes and fry in a little olive oil (they'll try to soak up a lot) until they are taking a little colour. Cool, bag up and use later, or simply toss into a green salad.

## DAY 7

# Breadcrumbs

Probably beginning to crack a little as the interior dries and shrinks. Grate, either by hand on a coarse cheese grater or in a food processor. Bag and freeze. Or stir a little olive oil through the crumbs with your fingers and use to top a vegetable casserole.

# Grow your own

People who grow their own food are often highly knowledgeable. There are plenty of accomplished allotment holders and gardeners out there, but any of us can give it a go. Growing food is something we have done for thousands of years and we are all capable.

When I moved from the Welsh countryside back to the city, I became aware of the difficulties that confront urban dwellers, the main one being space. With my keen gardener's eye I was noticing weeds sprouting in cracks in the pavement, herbs on the balconies of tower blocks and tomato plants on doorsteps. It reminded me of what can be grown in even the smallest of spaces.

Initially, to get a sense of your growing options and what space you have available, ask yourself the following:

**What size container can I fit in my space?**
— A simple plant pot, a window box, a raised bed?

**What conditions does my space offer?**
— Is it sheltered from wind?
— Does it get much sun?
— Is there water nearby?

**Do I have any decent soil?**

Generally, unless you have been fortunate to inherit well-loved raised beds or garden plots full of dark earthworm-rich compost, there will be work to do! Chances are you'll find soil that has one or many of the following problems: rocks, clods, waterlogging, compaction, cracking, weed cover.

Soil suffers if it is not looked after, especially if it is left bare. The main problems are compaction, erosion and lack of fertility — through not replacing organic matter taken out at harvest.

Remember the law of return. In other words, as you harvest your produce, remember to replenish the soil with plenty of decent compost. Make the most of the space that you do have by thinking about soil depth, as well as area. In fact, having a small space can be a blessing as you are forced to focus your energy efficiently. Nurturing a small area rather than fretting about taking on the earth will allow you to improve the soil and, in turn, your bounty.

In this way small can be intensive, productive, sustainable and beautiful.

# Courgettes

I have a love for courgette plants. With their large Gauguin-like leaves they offer good weed cover and are quick and easy to grow. Their only difficulty is the kind of problem I like: managing to eat them all.

I always grow a few varieties offering yellow, striped and the traditional sleek dark green. Courgette plants can use up a fair amount of space but they are definitely worth it! Try the fruit at different sizes. They will have a firmer texture when small. If picked late, they become large and can be cooked like marrows, stuffed or made into marrow and ginger jam or chutney.

Courgettes, and indeed all of the Cucurbitae family, produce wonderful, edible flowers. Fragile and beautiful, they perish to the touch so it is rare to find them for sale. They simply would not survive the supermarket regime. Courgette flowers are lovely stuffed and deep-fried or simply torn into salads for colour and their delicate flavour.

## Sowing method

Sow in pots of approx. 30 cm in diameter (or large enough to take at least two handfuls of potting compost).

**Conditions and timing**

Under cover from April to early June.

## Planting out

**Timing**

From mid May.

**Spacing**

Approx. 70 cm apart.

## Harvest

June to early October.

## Tips

— Sow seeds so they sit vertically in the soil. This reduces the chance of them rotting before germination.
— If planted out in a particularly cold May, the plants may benefit from a horticultural fleece cover.

## Trouble-shooting

— From August, leaves may suffer from mildew. Don't worry, as they will continue to produce fruit, but if it's severe simply prune affected leaves.
— Though hardy, these are exotic plants that do not like the cold. Production will slow and they will be killed after the first autumnal frosts. Leave in as ground cover that will break down over winter.
— Once planted out I undersow plants with green manures such as white clover or trefoil. Simply scatter seed over the area, water and firm in.

## Soulmates

— Olive oil, salt, pepper, goats' cheese, basil, garlic.

# Cucumbers

Cucumbers are part of the same family as courgettes so can be raised in a similar way. They are, like courgettes, exotic plants and need warmth to germinate and survive. They like sheltered, moist conditions so do best under cover — ideally in a greenhouse. If this isn't an option, make sure you choose an outdoor variety.

Cucumbers are prolific and produce large amounts of fruit from a few plants. They are a good source of vitamin C and other beneficial minerals when eaten fresh. Cucumber pickles (see page 259) are absolutely delicious and versatile, good with cheese, meats and fish.

## Tips

— Fruits are mainly made up of water so require lots while growing! Increase how much you water as the season goes on.

— Vining varieties can grow very tall so will need canes or strings to grow up for support. If they reach its top, they can be trained back down.

— When buying seed try to obtain indoor, all-female, hybrid F1 varieties for the most consistent yields.

— Check all chosen varieties are female. If not, remove male flowers (those without fruit), because if female flowers are pollinated the resulting fruit will be bitter.

— Cucumber stems are brittle so may break easily.

— Be especially careful when picking fruit so you don't damage the plant. I find it best to use a knife.

— If cucumbers get too large they will be tough, but can still be peeled or pickled.

— Outdoor cucumbers have tougher, bumpier skin and are also good pickled.

— Dill makes a good companion plant to repel red spider mites, which are prone to attacking cucumbers.

## Trouble-shooting

— Cucumbers are vulnerable to slugs when small but starting off under cover should offer protection.

— By late summer mildew tends to coat the underneath of larger leaves. Remove such leaves and plants will usually continue to bear fruit.

— Chopped comfrey leaves mixed with water and left for a few weeks make a potash-rich 'tea' that can be diluted and watered in to give plants a boost.

— Yellowing of lower leaves and tiny cobwebs are a sign of red spider mite. If it does get established, buy phytoseiulus (another mite that preys on the red spider mite).

— Cucumbers and all squash can be undersown with white clover or trefoil.

## Soulmates

— Dill, salt, pepper, olive oil, feta, vinegars, yoghurt, mint.

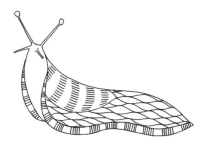

# Courgette relish

*Most people I know who have a garden get a week or two during the summer where things just go BOOM. Courgettes seem to be one of those things that come in abundance all at once. This is a great recipe for using up any gluts and also works well with marrows in place of courgette. I like my relish to be chunky so I dice the vegetables, but you could grate them or pulse them in a food processor if you prefer a finer texture.*

## Ingredients

**Makes approx. 1¾ litres**

—

1kg courgettes, diced finely
1 large onion, diced finely
1 tsp salt
500g green bell peppers, diced finely
750ml (3 cups) apple cider vinegar
150g light brown sugar
1 tsp turmeric
2 tsp celery seeds

Store in a cool, dark place.
Keeps well for up to one year.
Once opened, store in the fridge
and eat within two months.

## Method

Place the courgettes and onion into a colander, sprinkle with salt, mix with your hands and stand them over a bowl for an hour to drain off some of the excess liquid. There is no need to rinse the salt off after draining.

Combine all the ingredients in a large saucepan and bring to the boil, stirring occasionally to dissolve the sugar. Once boiling, turn down the heat and simmer for 30 minutes.

Ladle the relish, boiling hot, into hot sterilised jars, tap them down on the work surface to bring any air bubbles up to the surface and seal immediately.

# Cucumber pickles

*In America, the classic bread and butter pickles (known as cucumber pickles in the UK) have a kick of heat and are sweet rather than sour. I prefer mine sourer rather than sweet because I grew up with the German version, called Senfgurken (mustard cucumbers). This recipe combines the best of both worlds — spicy, sour and a little sweet. In place of the usual sugar I use honey. Great eaten with cheese and cold meats as a simple lunch.*

## Ingredients
**Makes approx. 1½ litres**

—

**1kg cucumbers**
  **(roughly 2 large ones)**
**100g shallots (approx. 4)**
**3 tsp salt**
**1 tsp celery seeds**
**2 tsp mustard seeds**
**½ tsp chilli flakes (optional)**
**1 tsp coriander seeds**
**4 bay leaves**
**1 tsp turmeric**
**500ml cider vinegar**
**150ml (⅔ cup) honey**

This will keep well for six months in a cool, dark place. Once opened, store in the fridge and use within two months.

## Method
Peel the cucumbers and cut in half lengthways, scrape out the seeds with a spoon and discard. Cut into ½ cm thick half moons. Slice the shallots in half and then into thin slices. Place both into a colander over a bowl, sprinkle with salt, toss with your hands and leave to drain for two hours.

Rinse the cucumber and shallots in cold water to remove the salt. Combine the remaining ingredients in a large saucepan and bring to the boil, stirring to dissolve the honey. Add the cucumbers and shallots, turn down the heat and cook for 5 minutes — do not allow to boil.

Pack into hot sterilised jars (make sure there is one bay leaf per jar) and seal immediately.

# Keep growing

Working on the land has come to be perceived as being far removed from all that is cultural and creative in much of modern society. With industrialisation, diversity is replaced by monoculture, people are replaced by machines and we are increasingly separated from the land that sustains us. It is an efficient system but one that can have many hidden costs.

Sometimes the work is very hard and you can feel very small in a system where appreciation and pay can be low, but there is another side. The moments of wonder at the beauty around you; having the privilege to witness the detail of nature. I have found my best thoughts happen when working at a steady rhythm in a place where I am immersed in the natural world. There is a pervasive idea that bypassing the need for hard and repetitive work is meant to free humans to become more happy, intellectual and creative beings. Obviously there is a balance, but physical work can create engagement, and engagement is central to our experience of life. When my work is physical, I sleep well, have an appetite and my worries fade away.

Agriculture is the foundation stone of human civilisation and I feel it should not be seen as something separate from our cerebral life. We are not separate from nature. Food is a point where humans connect.

## A note on organic methods

When my parents first moved to Wales they wanted to come up with a system of farming that looked after the land and cycled resources as much as possible. In doing so, it would be sustainable for the future. This resulted in them and others drawing up some standards to enable this to happen in a way that was visible. The organic movement was attempting to enable the public to have control over how we look after the environment and what we eat. At their bare bones these standards are what we have come to know as the organic standard today.

What we put onto our land affects what we put into our bodies. My parents recognised that soil was at the heart of maintaining the health of the whole. Whatever guises organic has taken, I always come back to this interconnection between soil, body and environment. To understand the world around us, we tend to break it down, but in doing so there is a danger of losing a sense of our wider relationships and how we interconnect.

Soil is a resource that we are fundamentally connected to. It is the source of almost all our food. Keeping soil fertile needs to be done in a way that protects it for the future. Feeding soil through the addition of nitrogen-chemical fertiliser is a wholly unsustainable practice that our conventional farming system relies too heavily upon. It pollutes and uses up world oil capital at a rapid rate.

Organic growing focuses on looking after your soil as a whole rather than applying quick fixes for things that may be deficient or cause disease. Soil needs to be nurtured otherwise it can be damaged or even lost through compaction, pollution, erosion or salination. In the UK we stand to lose five tonnes of top-soil per hectare per year because of the way we farm. This is wasting soil reserves, a legacy that took thousands of years to build. We are using up a gift that does not solely belong to us.

The other secret held by our seemingly humble soil is that it is a massive carbon sink, holding more carbon even than our oceans. Cultivating soil allows the oxidation of carbon, which contributes to climate change. Organic systems try to minimise the release of carbon and instead focus on returning carbon to the soil (in the form of organic matter: compost and plants). In doing this we can slow down climate change while also improving the structure and fertility of this vital resource. This all may sound a little complex and you may be thinking, 'How does this relate to me and my patch?' Really it is about being conscious of our place in the larger system and we can do this from anywhere. If we harvest food from our gardens we can abide by the law of return. Composting organic waste converts it into something that is useful.

––––––––

In a world where we have become increasingly detached from our food source, buying organically certified food is a way of gaining control over the systems we support. It is a legal term — unlike 'fresh', 'local', etc. — so it is regulated. However, the need for the legislation of 'organic' food is also in part a symptom of us having accepted detachment from the food we eat.

We can all reconnect and challenge this separation by forging more direct connections, with local farms and farmers and through the way we choose to shop. Or by growing things ourselves.

The beauty of a farmers' market, box schemes and community-supported agriculture is you can talk directly to the producers, ask questions and even visit the farms. I share the view of Mr Woody Guthrie: 'This land is your land, and this land is my land.' We are all responsible and more powerful than we think. We steward the land in the choices we make every time we eat.

# THE 10 COMMANDMENTS OF A GROWER

1 **Diversity builds health**

2 **Diversity builds resilience**

3 **Remember the law of return** — compost and cycle fertility

4 **Think for the future** — invest in the soil and sow for the next season

5 **Observe nature** — you will learn as you 'Do'

6 **Use what you have** — make waste useful and use the resources on your doorstep

7 **Adapt to your context** — both its advantages and disadvantages

8 **Water is life** — try to harness and preserve this precious resource

9 **Nurture your soil** and it will nurture you

10 **Food is the way to people's hearts**

**EPILOGUE**

# The most natural thing in the world

Improvising is the most natural thing in the world. We all do it. You are doing it now. Your eyes, skin, gut, blood and brain are all improvising, each on their own and all together. Like a forest, or traffic on our roads, or email traffic on the internet, or the food supply to New York City, the most stupendously complex flows are organised in a wonderfully intricate, improvised dance. There is no one in control. The global pandemic of 2020 brought this home in no uncertain terms.

Understanding this is a fabulous liberation. In the past, when most of what happened was way beyond our understanding, the dogged pursuit of control made sense. But not anymore.

I once ran a course called 'Sit Stretch Eat Play' with my friend Edward Espe Brown, which combined meditation, yoga, cooking and improv (hence the name). After meditation one day, Ed was musing on the question of control, which someone had raised: 'It's a funny thing to want really, isn't it ... Because you could never achieve it, and even if you could ... Well, wouldn't that be dull.'

The promise that once we get everything ticked off and tidied up, then we can be happy, is a delusion, and a dull one at that. Who would want such a life? This doesn't mean giving up a way of thinking that has been so successful, but it does mean understanding its limits. A plan, or script, or recipe will only get you so far. There are other intelligent responses that complement our existing approach. Improvisation is one of them. It doesn't just help you navigate the mess. It is a way to happily be in it.

Taking to heart a few simple ideas that improv offers us can shift how we go about our everyday lives and work. They help us to accept, with humility, that we play a small part in an incomprehensibly complex world. They help us to enjoy what uncertainty brings us, rather than always trying to close it down.

They give us some ideas about how we can hold ourselves while we move towards 'the more beautiful world our hearts know is possible',* which we cannot yet see, or describe. They enable us to reconnect with our own irreducible, improvisational nature and, most importantly, give us something practical and simple to do.

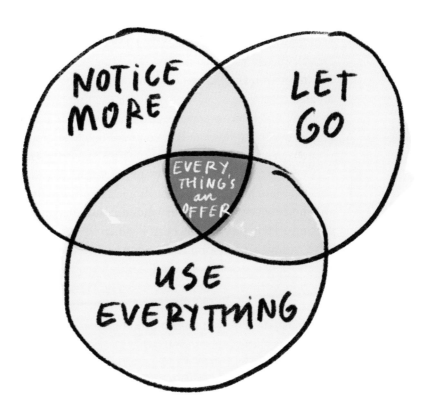

* The More Beautiful World Our Hearts Know is Possible by Charles Eisenstein

# What gives our life meaning?

The pursuit of happiness often ignores that other emotions like sadness, anger, vulnerability or jealousy are integral to the human experience. It's yin and yang, light and dark, you can't have one without the other; even a black hole has light in it. Good and bad experiences give your life meaning and create opportunities for growth and transformation. It's a bit like grief. All you can really do is surrender to and honour that emotional pain and suffering until it passes. Denying negative feelings doesn't make them go away, they just find another way to show up in your life as either physical symptoms or suppression that can manifest in addictive behaviour.

In her TED talk 'There's More to Life Than Being Happy' Emily Esfahani Smith asks, 'Can chasing happiness make people unhappy?' She describes happiness as feeling good in a moment whereas having meaning in your life is long-lasting and makes you think about others and being your better self.

Not only can meaning be found in human connection and creating a new story for yourself, you can also find it in having experiences that transcend the everyday. These experiences bring clarity, perspective and inspiration. Things like yoga, meditation, art, music, exercise, singing, or attending a religious or spiritual gathering. Anything that makes you feel like you are connected to something bigger than you can be meaningful. It might spark you to dream, create, imagine or just be. I went on a yoga retreat at a time when I was trying to come up with a name for a new venture. It was at the end of a session during *savasana* (the relaxing bit) that I saw the words 'Doing Death' in my mind embedded within an image of the solar system. I had been trying to think of a name for months! But in that moment of space and transcendence I had utter clarity.

Most people on their deathbed don't say they wish they had worked more. But work is a big part of your life, so make it count. Try and do something you enjoy, get paid for it, and if you don't love it, see if you can change it. Make time to do something to help and inspire others. Find something that matters to you, find your purpose, find contentment.

## Death as a teacher

Often, when I step outside the hospice after a shift I have the sensation that I am experiencing things differently. I notice the clouds in the sky, the light reflecting on leaves, the wind on my face. It's a curious feeling. Our day-to-day lives are just as important as what we strive for. I hold my children a little tighter on those days and I feel grateful. An awareness of death has given me an appreciation for the simple things in life.

It's not practical to live each day as if it's your last, but you could try to spend one day with this mindset. How might that make you feel? A day filled with micro-moments that count. Perhaps you'd tell those close to you what they mean to you. You might have more of an acceptance of your own and others' flaws. Or be less bothered by the challenges that the day brings. Maybe you'd be less self-conscious, or be more authentic. It might prompt you to be kinder and more compassionate to those around you.

Death gives life clarity. It allows you to live more in the present and be able to see the everyday beauty in people and experiences. If your head spends too much time in the future or retreating into the past, you forget to live in the present, with your heart.

# What's your legacy?

Phew, you made it! Here we are. This is it. The big one. The final piece of advice I can give you. Ready? Right then.

## MAKE THINGS THAT MATTER SO YOU CAN LEAVE THEM BEHIND FOR OTHERS.

That sounds very grand, doesn't it? And it should, because it's such a powerful thing to be able to leave your imprint for others to discover and build on. We can all do it.

I want this statement to make you feel strong and powerful, inspired to do great things, but I also want it to feel realistic. You should make and do things that matter to you, that can be left behind — for your dog, your own kids, or the entire human race … it's up to you.

Your success and your goals are exactly that, yours. We'd all love to change the world, save the environment, revolutionise education, solve poverty and famine — and for some people that is their goal and their path, and that is their legacy. But just because you want to start an origami business in Warwick because you love the art of folding paper, don't let the comparison of scale make you feel like that's any less impactful. That's your path and that will be your legacy. We'll all be helping the world collectively if we passionately, positively and honestly live our lives, pursuing the things that matter to us.

Happiness is a universal currency; a smile is understood the world over. If what you do makes someone grin uncontrollably, then that is a very powerful thing; don't underestimate the value of it. If we could all encourage a little more grinning and a bit less grimacing, then we'd be changing the world in the process too!

What matters even more is what your legacy should be as a person, what you bring to the world as an individual. Your projects, pursuits and passions speak volumes, but that's because they're a natural extension of you as a human being. Be kind, be humble, be honest, be open, be supportive, be compassionate, be patient, be engaged, be excited, be dedicated, be true, be absolutely lovely. Be all of these things and more, because that's the real mark of success.

There's a film that I've loved since I was young but only when I watched it again as an adult did I realise that it features the most inspirational and honest message in its closing scene. Impressive really when you consider it's a 1976 musical gangster film featuring a cast of child actors (with adult singing voices). Yep, you guessed it, *Bugsy Malone*! And it feels like the perfect way to end the book. 'Why?' I hear you cry with confusion. Because it feels totally fitting to take our last inspirational words from a film that's full of energy and heart, with the wonderfully silly situation of children masquerading as grown-ups, trying to make their way in the world.

So I'll leave you with this, because never a truer word has been said...

# YOU GIVE
# A LITTLE
# LOVE
# AND IT
# ALL COMES
# BACK
# TO YOU

# YOU'RE GONNA BE REMEMBERED FOR THE THINGS THAT YOU SAY AND DO

# ENJOY THE RIDE, IT'S YOUR RIDE

Deal with each day one day at a time. Don't dwell on the past. Don't live in the future. Keep working in the now. Head down. Working on the thing that matters to you. Stay in the now.

Don't spend your time moaning. Be thankful for each day. And enjoy the ride. It's your ride. You are making the decisions. Get your mind looking for the positives and not the negatives. Surround yourself with people who take you up and not bring you down.

Even the hardest days you will have, you will look back on with a smile.

# TIME FOR A DRINK

EPILOGUE

# Cassis

*A beautiful vivid liquor evocative of summer. Tasty drizzled over ice cream, in sorbets or best of all pour a little into white wine for a 'Kir' or sparkling white wine for a 'Kir Royale' — delicious.*

## Ingredients

**Makes roughly 1 litre**

—

**500g blackcurrants, freshly picked and checked through**
**500ml brandy or vodka**
**200g granulated sugar**

## Method

Place the blackcurrants into a jar and cover with the brandy (or vodka if you wish). Seal and leave in a cool, dark place for at least 6 weeks.

Strain the blackcurrants through a muslin and keep the liquor. Mix the blackcurrant liquor with the sugar in the bottle you will finally store it in.

Shake the mixture twice a day until the sugar is fully dissolved. Sugar here is a matter of taste — you might want to use a bit more or less, so try once it's made.

This will keep for up to one year in a cool, dark cupboard.

# Rhubarb gin

*This is a simple and also quite sophisticated way of capturing the fresh tang of rhubarb in a bottle. It's lovely to sip on its own, for a G&T with a difference, or as an addition to a cocktail for a bit of fun.*

## Ingredients

**Makes 500ml**

—

**250g rhubarb (the pinker the better) chopped into 1.5cm pieces**
**400ml (1¾ cups) gin**
**120g granulated sugar**

## Method

Put the fruit in a jar, and completely cover with gin. Store in a cool, dark place for 1 week.

Strain the mixture through a muslin, reserving the liquid. Pour it, with the sugar, back into the bottle. A funnel might be useful. Shake the bottle every day until the sugar is dissolved.

Your gin is ready to enjoy — just add ice and tonic!

Store in a cool, dark place and drink within the year.

# Blueberry, mint and lime cordial

*Fruity and zesty, this cordial packs a real punch.*

### Ingredients

**Makes approx. 1 litre**

—

**500ml lime juice**
**(approx. 16 limes)**
**30 mint leaves**
**500g blueberries**
**650g sugar**
**500ml water**

### Method

Put all the ingredients into a saucepan and bring to the boil, stirring occasionally to dissolve the sugar. Boil for 10 minutes (no more, otherwise you will be making a jelly).

Pour the syrup through a sieve to separate the blueberries and mint leaves.

Bottle in sterilised jars while still hot. Seal and allow to cool before storing in the fridge.

This will keep for a month.
Note: Don't throw away the blueberries, mix them with some apples and use them in a pie.

# About the authors

**Amanda Blainey**

Amanda Blainey is the founder of Doing Death, a multimedia platform and podcast that opens up more authentic conversations about death and dying. She works with patients in a UK hospice and is training to be a death doula. She is the author of *Do Death* (2019).

**Bobette Buster**

Bobette Buster is the writer/producer of an award-winning feature documentary, TEDx speaker and Professor of Storytelling. She is a story consultant to major studios including Pixar, Disney and Sony Animation. She is the author of *Do Story* (2013) and *Do Listen* (2018).

**Libby DeLana**

Libby DeLana is an award-winning creative director who has spent her thirty-year career in advertising. In 2011, she took a morning walk and hasn't missed a day since. She is founder of ThisMorningWalk™ and co-host of the *This Morning Walk* podcast with Alex Elle. She is the author of *Do Walk* (2021).

**Tim Drake**

Tim Drake has co-founded and run businesses, think tanks and charities. He is the author of several books, including *Do Agile* (2020). He has seen success and failure in business over four decades, and has learned from both.

**Anja Dunk, Jen Goss & Mimi Beaven**

Anja Dunk is a cook, author and artist. She grew up in the Welsh countryside where homegrown produce and wild foraging were part of daily life. Jen Goss lives on a smallholding in west Wales and runs catering company Our Two Acres. Mimi Beaven lives in the Hudson Valley, New York, where she teaches cookery classes. Combining their culinary experience, the three friends wrote *Do Preserve* in 2016.

**Sue Fan & Danielle Quigley**

Sue Fan and Danielle Quigley are photographers and designers who strive to live a wilder and more beautiful life. Together they created Wild Habit, a lifestyle brand that takes inspiration from nature. They have created installations for large corporations, styled for The DO Lectures, and have a retail space in Oceanside, California. They wrote *Do Inhabit* in 2018.

## Orren Fox

Orren Fox is a beekeeper who has taken part in a 'Honey Showdown' at the White House, a longboard builder and economics graduate. When he gave his DO Lecture in 2012, he was just 15 years old. He is the author of *Do Beekeeping* (2015).

## Lucy Gannon

When Lucy Gannon was nearly 40, she entered (and won!) a playwriting competition. It was the first play she had ever written. She went on to become one of Britain's most successful screenwriters. In 1997 she was awarded an MBE for services to television drama. She is the author of *Do Drama* (2022).

## Charlie Gladstone

Charlie Gladstone is an entrepreneur, retailer, festival owner, farmer, author, podcast host, property developer and charity board member. His small businesses employ over 100 people and include The Good Life Society, the Hawarden Estate Farm Shop and Glen Dye Cabins and Cottages. He is the author of *Do Team* (2021).

## Tom Herbert

Tom is a fifth-generation baker and one half of TV's Fabulous Baker Brothers. In 2018, he founded community food hall and social enterprise The Long Table, supporting food hubs and local supply chains around Gloucestershire. He is the author of *Do Wild Baking* (2017).

## David Hieatt

Based in west Wales, David Hieatt is co-founder of The DO Lectures and Hiut Denim. He has a cult internet following and has spoken at Apple, Google and Red Bull, amongst others. He is the author of *Do Purpose* (2014), *Do Open* (2017) and *The Path of a Doer* (2010).

## Alice Holden

Alice Holden is head grower at Growing Communities, an urban organic farm and social enterprise in East London. She is the author of *Do Grow* (2013).

## Les McKeown

Les McKeown is the President of Predictable Success, advising CEOs and senior managers on leadership and how to achieve scalable, sustainable growth. Based in Washington DC, Les spends his time consulting, writing and speaking. His books include *Do Lead* (2014), *Do Scale* (2019) and *WSJ* bestseller *Predictable Success*.

## Alison, David & Jess Lea-Wilson

Alison and David Lea-Wilson started Halen Môn, the Anglesey Sea Salt company, in 1997. They have always made a living from the sea, first as fishmongers then aquarium owners, and in 2019, were awarded MBEs for their services to business — the same year they wrote *Do Sea Salt* with their daughter, Jess.

## Alan Moore

Alan Moore is an author, speaker and craftsman of beautiful businesses. He mentors teams and individuals, delivers leadership programmes and advises clients on regenerative business practices. He is the author of *Do Design* (2016) and *Do Build* (2020).

## Tamsin Omond

Tamsin Omond is an inspirational climate leader and the author of *Do Earth* (2021). Highly skilled in building environmental and social justice campaigns and strategy, Tamsin works with organisations and leads public conversations on the climate and ecological emergency.

## James Otter

James Otter is the founder of Otter Surfboards, where he designs and makes award-winning wooden surfboards. He has also led workshop courses for the past eight years, sharing his passion for making with others, and is the author of *Do Make* (2020).

## Andrew Paynter

Andrew Paynter is a photographer and director based in Oakland, California. His clients include Coca-Cola, Adidas, Levi's, Apple and Rolling Stone. He has embarked on several decade-long photographic collaborations, including with artist Geoff McFetridge. He is the author of *Do Photo* (2020).

## Robert Poynton

Robert Poynton is an Associate Fellow of the Saïd Business School and the founder of Yellow, an online learning experience. He divides his time between Oxford and a small town in rural Spain. He is the author of *Do Improvise* (2013) and *Do Pause* (2019).

## Mark Shayler

Mark Shayler runs Ape, an innovation and sustainability consultancy. He helps big companies think small and small companies think big. He is a keynote speaker, leads Qigong sessions and is the author of *Do Disrupt* (2017) and *Do Present* (2020).

## James Sills

James Sills is the founder of The Sofa Singers, an open-access online choir formed during the 2020 pandemic that received global news coverage. He is passionate about helping people feel good through singing and runs various community choirs and corporate workshops. He is the author of *Do Sing* (2019).

## Gavin Strange

Gavin Strange is a director and designer at Aardman Animations, the Academy Award-winning studio behind *Shaun the Sheep* and *Wallace & Gromit*. A keynote speaker and the author of *Do Fly* (2016), he is a great believer in passion projects and develops his own under the moniker Jamfactory.

## Michael Townsend Williams

From a life of 'doing' in the world of advertising to a life of 'being' as a yoga, breathwork and meditation teacher, Michael Townsend Williams now works on the integration of both. He coaches amazing individuals, teams and brands around the world, and is the author of *Do Breathe* (2015).

## Andrew Whitley

Andrew Whitley has been an organic baker for over four decades and has 'changed the way we think about bread' (BBC Food & Farming Award judges). Based in Scotland, he now runs Scotland The Bread, a collaborative project to grow better grain and bake better bread. He is the author of *Do Sourdough* (2014).

# Picture credits

The publishers would like to thank the copyright holders below for their kind permission to reproduce their work in *The Book of Do*.

Corresponding page numbers are given below, and the Do Book that features the image.

1. Tom Etherington, based on artworks by James Victore
4–5. Dom Francis Pellegrino, *Do Walk*
6. Andrew Paynter, *Do Photo*
8. Miranda West, The DO Lectures, 2017
11. Gavin Strange, *Do Fly*
12–13. Andrew Paynter, *Do Purpose*
14. Andrew Paynter, *Do Photo*
16–17. Gavin Strange, *Do Fly*
28–29, 34–35. Andrew Paynter, *Do Purpose*
36. Hannah Cousins, *Do Wild Baking*
40–41. Jim Marsden, *Do Pause*
45. Nick Hand, *Do Grow*
52–53, 60–61. Andrew Paynter, *Do Photo*
65. Gavin Strange, *Do Fly*
66. Andy Smith, *Path of a Doer*
67. Olaf Ladousse, *Do Purpose*
69. Andy Smith, *Path of a Doer*
72–3. Andrew Paynter, *Do Photo*
74–5. Nick Hand, *Do Grow*
76–7. Andrew Paynter, *Do Purpose*
85, 86, 89, 91. Olaf Ladousse, *Do Purpose*
92–3. Andrew Paynter, *Do Purpose*
94–95. James Otter, *Do Make*
97. Gavin Strange, *Do Fly*
102–103. Laurent Nivalle, *Do Design*
109. Hannah Cousins, *Do Sing*
112–3, 114–5. Andrew Paynter, *Do Purpose*
116, 121. Matt Blease, *Do Team*
122–3, 126–7. Andrew Paynter, *Do Purpose*
129. Millie Marotta, *Do Lead*

132. Andrew Paynter, *Do Open*
134, 137, 138. Matt Blease, *Do Team*
145. Sue Parkhill, *Do Death*
149. Hannah Cousins, *Do Wild Baking*
152. Andrew Paynter, *Do Photo*
158. Mat Arney, *Do Make*
163. James Victore, *Do Build*
164. Andrew Paytner, *Do Photo*
171. Jim Marsden, *Do Pause*
175, 179. Millie Marotta, *Do Story*
176. Andrew Paynter, *Do Purpose*
184–5. Mat Arney
191. Jonathan Cherry, *Do Breathe*
195. Michael Piazza, *Do Walk*
196–7, 201, 202, 206–7. Libby DeLana, *Do Walk*
208–9. Alice Aedy, *Do Earth*
212. Julian Calverley, *Do Build*
220–1. Michael Piazza, *Do Beekeeping*
224–5. Jonathan Cherry, *Do Sourdough*
226–7, 228. Jody Daunton, *Do Wild Baking*
231, 232, 235. Hannah Cousins, *Do Wild Baking*
233, 234. Jody Daunton, *Do Wild Baking*
236–7. Sue Fan, *Do Inhabit*
239, 241, 244. Jeska & Dean Hearne, *Do Inhabit*
247. Hannah Cousins, *Do Wild Baking*
248–51. Jonathan Cherry, *Do Sourdough*
253. Hannah Cousins, *Do Wild Baking*
254, 256. Nick Hand, *Do Grow*
255, 257. Millie Marotta, *Do Grow*
264–5. Haarala Hamilton, *Do Sea Salt*
267. Nick Parker, *Do Improvise*
274. Andrew Paynter, *Do Photo*
276–7. Mickey Smith, *Do Breathe*
278. Richard Beaven, *Do Preserve*
279. Hannah Cousins, *Do Wild Baking*
280, 281. Richard Beaven, *Do Preserve*
282–3. Sue Parkhill, *Do Death*

# Books in the series

Available in print, digital and audio formats from booksellers
or via our website: *thedobook.co*. To hear about events
and forthcoming titles, you can find us on social media
@*dobookco*, or subscribe to our newsletter